TRI-VIA SERMONS
for Lenten
Reflection & Renewal

BY
ROBERT R. GILLOGLY, PH.D.

Asterisk Publications
Peoria, IL   1993

Previous Asterisk Publications
by the author include:

DISCERNING THE SPIRIT OF LIFE IN MAKING
DECISIONS ABOUT DEATH

FOR PETE'S SAKE!

For further information, please address:

Asterisk Publications
P.O. Box 3108
Peoria, Illinois 61612-3108

Printed By
Art & Print Co.
Washington, IL   1993

TABLE OF CONTENTS

INTRODUCTION:
THE ENCOMPASSING CROSS
—A MATTER OF TIME

While in college as a student wrestling with the prospects of entering the ministry, a good pastor friend and mentor, the Episcopalian rector in my hometown, died. He left me many memories as well as his library. Among H. Foster Whitney's many volumes were some delightful books designed for Lenten reflection and renewal. Other denominations also publish study guides for church members and congregational use during Lent, but I remember those 'presiding bishop's' books best. It probably had a lot to do with their special connection to Father Whitney's example. He also gave me the best advice any aspiring minister could ever receive. At his kitchen table, while sharing a light lunch once, he casually dropped this one on me.

> "Remember Bob, people are going to talk anyway.
> Your job is to give them something good to talk about!"

That is what I hope this book will do, provide people who read it with "something good to talk about." Another of his remarks I try to remember— I should, because he said it more than once was,

> "And don't forget to preach Christ,…and Him crucified."

As I hope you will discover, this book intends to address *"THE ENCOMPASSING CROSS"* as it literally incorporates time and in particular—our time. For many people sermons ipso facto are trivial—which is obviously an uninformed perspective—Cough! Cough! These are *TRI-VIA* sermons and there is an important difference. I am well aware of the fact that for the general public and even for many in the pews, "trivia sermons" constitutes a tautology, the kind of pleonastic language critics expect from the church and from people who frequent such places and use such phrases as "free grace, past history, future hope.…"

Moreover, whereas admittedly many sermons are a waste of time, these sermons are about time. I am reminded of the ancient Greek *adiaphora*, a term which variously meant "Insignificant things, matters of indifference,

1

neither good nor bad, little nothing things." Or, if you prefer the Latin language used by attorneys, *de minimus*, which, when translated, means "negligible, insignificant, inconsequential," in short, "beneath my dignity as a lawyer to consider. " These **TRI-VIA** sermons are neither trivial, adiaphora or de minimus, they are important, because they purport to take us to the center of *"THE ENCOMPASSING CROSS—A MATTER OF TIME."*

My point of departure is the conflation of two texts: I Corinthians 13:13 and John 14:6. As Jaroslav Pelikan has pointed out, "the relation among faith, hope, and charity has long engaged the attention of Christian theology.[1] Even more so when "the way, the truth and the life" are included. To a certain extent these sermons represent what could be called, "temporal theology," an attempt to take seriously the temporal implications of the encompassing cross.

Time—something which we either have too much or too little of. "Time" is "the ultimate scarcity," wrote Wilbert Moore. He bemoaned the fact that there are many ways of talking about space and social behavior, for example, ecology and demography, but "the temporal ordering of social behavior has received only sporadic or intermittent attention by the sciences dealing with human beings.[2] In fact, he added that there is not even a "name for a science of the temporal dimensions of social life." Fortunately, in our own time "time" is receiving more scientific attention as evidenced by Stephen W. Hawking's *A Brief History of Time—From the Big Bang to Black Holes*.[3]

In our clock conscious society in particular, time literally flies, frequently passing us by before we have "taken time" to think about our temporality. Salvador Dali, the surrealist artist, has given us a phantasmagoric illustration entitled, "The Persistence of Memory."[4] Grotesquely misshapen clocks and smashed timepieces are seen strewn about a barren landscape, so brilliantly capturing our human tragedy, the realization that our time is soon consumed, what Shakespeare once called, "devouring time" (Sonnet IX).

Jonathan Swift (1667-1745), probably most renowned as the author of *Gulliver's Travels*, was preoccupied with time and seems to have been describing our modern dilemma also when he wrote,

> *"Time*
> *Ever eating, never cloying,*
> *All-devouring, all destroying*
> *Never finding full repast*
> *Till I eat the world at last."*[5]

Similarly, a parishioner in making her funeral arrangements recently gave me memorable lines from an anonymous author her 5th grade teacher had quoted in a cherished autograph book. She asked that I include them in her memorial service,

> *The clock of life is wound but once.*
> *But no man has the power*
> *To tell just when the hands will stop*
> *At late or early hour.*
> *Now is the only time we own.*
> *Live, love, work with a will.*
> *Have no faith in tomorrow*
> *For the hands may then be still.*

The primary **TRI-VIA** sermons around which this little book is structured are Chapters 1, 5, 9, and the Epilogue. The remaining chapters further illustrate the central themes of this book summarized by "The Truth of Faith," "The Way of Hope," and "The Life of Love."

It is amazing how other New Testament texts both illustrate the **TRI-VIA**. while adding new possibilities for further Lenten R & R:

> "We give thanks to God always for you all, constantly mentioning you in our prayers, remembering before our God and Father your work of **FAITH**, and labor of **LOVE** and steadfastness of **HOPE** in our Lord Jesus Christ." (I Thessalonians 2:16-17)

> "Let us draw near with a true heart in full assurance of **FAITH**, with our hearts sprinkled clean from an evil conscience and our bodies washed with pure water.
> Let us hold fast the confession of our **HOPE** without wavering, for He who promised is faithful;
> And let us consider how to stir up one another to **LOVE** and good works, not neglecting to meet together, as is the habit of some, but encouraging one another, and all the more as you see the Day drawing near." (Hebrews 10:22-25)

> "We always thank God, the Father of our Lord Jesus Christ, when we pray for you, because we have heard of your **FAITH** in Christ Jesus and of the **LOVE** which you have for all the saints, because of the **HOPE** laid up for you in heaven. Of this you have heard before in the word of the truth, the Gospel...." (Colossians 1:3-5)

Using the spiritual and temporal template on the following page allows us to consider some pretty tough theological topics like the Trinity in Chapter 1, Predestination in Chapter 5, Justice in Chapter 9 and Forgiveness in the Epilogue. In addition, there is the usual amount of illustrative miscellany included from contemporary culture, literature, history and philosophy and the kitchen sink—all the results of exploring and enjoying the spiritual mysteries of **THE ENCOMPASSING CROSS** and trying to come up with TRI-VIA for people to talk about.

Robert R. Gillogly
Peoria, 1993

PRAYER OF CONFESSION

Eternal God, we confess that we seldom sense the importance of time. When we do, it's usually not when we're on
time; but, when we're too late or too early, when we've
either wasted time or have too much time. Sometimes we
lose track of time; sometimes we try to make up for time
lost. Moreover, we seldom take time to do anything very
important, let alone be 'holy and speak oft with our God.'
We don't even take time to be human and speak oft with
each other. But most of all, we panic when we suddenly
realize how little time there is for any of us. Forgive us for
not taking our time seriously enough and for not enjoying
enough the time we have been given. Help us to take time
for those things that matter most in life, namely, other people. Help us to love one another as you have loved us in
Christ, for that is what time is all about. Amen.

TRI-VIA

PAST   PRESENT   FUTURE

Truth   **Way**
John 14:6

Life
Love

Faith   Hope
I Corinthians 13:13

Nothing that is worth doing can be achieved in our lifetime;
***Therefore we must be saved by* hope.**
Nothing which is true or beautiful or good makes complete sense in any immediate context of history;
***Therefore we must be saved by* faith.**
Nothing we do, however virtuous, can be accomplished alone.
***Therefore we are saved by* love.**
No virtuous act is quite as virtuous from the standpoint of our friend or foe as it is from our standpoint.
***Therefore we must be saved by the final form of love which is* forgiveness.**

Reinhold Niebuhr
(1892-1971)

PART I
– THE PAST –
FAITH and TRUTH

THE TRUTH OF FAITH

TRIVIA as we would normally use the term means something insignificant, of little consequence or value, something trifling, prattling, petty. But there is a far more suggestive meaning associated with the term that I want to explore with you this morning—and for a number of Sunday mornings in the months ahead. We will be using the term in its original Latin sense, namely, as a word that literally means the junction where three—*tri*—roads or ways—*via*—meet, to form a *trivium. TRIV-IA* means where three roads cross. Wherever such a crossroads exists, is a good spot for commerce, and a place where travelers can exchange the latest news and views and gossip. Hence *trivia* became equated with marketplace small-talk. But it is the convergence of three ways that is important for us, as we reflect literally on the *CROSS*-roads and-as you might imagine—more than one sense of the word *CROSS*. There is even more than double entendre intended.

Language can be fun and—as you know—always filled with sermon possibilities. The various uses of *tri* are well-known to us and *v-i-a*, pronounced either "vi-a" or "wee-a" when by itself means "by way of." Or, it can mean just a road or a way. Then there's *viator* meaning a wayfarer or traveller. Gabriel Marcel once wrote a wonderful book entitled *Homo Viator.*[1] Then there's viaduct or a roadway over a ravine and *via media* or the "middle way." There are many uses of *via*.

This sermon was delivered February 14, 1993 at First Federated Church, Peoria, Illinois. Scripture lessons were taken from Acts 5:20; 9:1-2; 19:8-10, 23; 22:4-5; 24:14-15, (cf. 22); 26:19 29.

In a more ecclesiastical sense the eucharist, when administered at the point of death or when one is in extreme danger, is called the *viaticum* or spiritual provisions for our final spiritual journey, even as the word in ancient Roman daily use meant food for official and routine earthly journeys. Then, finally, by way of via examples, in the near future we will again be following the *Via Dolorosa*, the way of the Cross, the road that took Jesus to Golgotha, a phrase which literally means, "the sorrowful way."

In the passages from Acts we read, we heard various references to the early Christians as "followers of the way." The language is central, because for Christians as for the earlier Israelites, it was God who revealed the way, showed the way, led the way.

The word for way in Greek is *"odos."* The central event of Old Testament history is the *EX – ODOS,* literally the way out of slavery, the way out of Egypt, God's deliverance of the Israelites. Having experienced the grace of that act of God—which the Israelites acknowledged as divine deliverance—they were obliged to live life thereafter according to God's WAY, which is what the TEN COMMANDMENTS represent.[2]

As Christians we have inherited *The Way of Israel.*[3] However, we are the recipients of a new way, the way of God revealed not on tablets or in the works of creation, rather in a person. Jesus Christ revealed to us the way or plan or purposes of God. In the Gospel according to Matthew, the Herodians and the Pharisees addressed Jesus,

"Teacher we know that *you are true* and *teach the way of God truthfully....*"[4]

Though intended as a set-up in order to trap Him, Jesus did reveal the way of God in human history and taught us *"the way of God truthfully."* But more than that *He became the Way.* In the Gospel according to John, Jesus was talking with Thomas who asked Him, "Lord, we do not know where we're going; how can we know the way?" Jesus said to Thomas,

"I am the way, and the truth and the life;...." (14:5-6)

10

His followers early on made claims that Jesus was the Christ and they became known as "followers of the way," for they identified Jesus personally with God's way. They believed God had been realized or actualized in Him and in history and in their presence.

They hadn't found the way. Ironically, in the words of the late Dag Hammarskjöld, "The Way had come to them,"[5] and as a consequence, they were no longer searching. They knew the way, because they knew Him. That is the secret, still unknown and unacknowledged by many people, but for us—well-known and absolutely indispensable for understanding and living life. When we acknowledge that the *truth* of God has come to us, when we accept for ourselves the reality of Christ as God's truth and place our trust in Him, that is *faith*. That experience makes us Christians, which is what the early "followers of the way" were soon called, "*Christians*."[6]

There are only three references to these "peculiar" people called *Christians* in the New Testament—once in I Peter (4:16) and twice in the Acts of the Apostles. In the eleventh chapter we learn that it was in Antioch that the disciples were first called *Christians* (11:26) and then in that interesting passage from the twenty-sixth chapter we read how Paul in defending himself before King Agrippa was accused of trying to make the king a *Christian*.

* * * * *

The point of all this is that the fact of Jesus, who is the Christ, is the starting point of our Christian faith; it is our spiritual beginning as Christians. We don't end with Jesus Christ. We start with Him, when we can accept Him for ourselves, when we believe that in Him is the truth of God revealed, not just generally, but for us personally. Thereafter we identify ourselves with Him and understand our story in terms of *His*-story. So for the Christian what is primary is our living experience of Jesus Christ. That basic commitment constitutes our spiritual birth, our Christian beginning.

So for the Christian *faith and truth* are PAST REALITIES based on what has already happened in *His*-story. Not only history in general is dated from that Christ-Event, split literally into halves, but our own *SPIRITUAL* history relates to the influence that event has had upon our lives. What we call *FAITH*, which is to say, the *TRUTH* about God, happened once for all in Jesus Christ. That is as some have suggested, our "cosmic prejudice." On the basis of that past reality we understand both our present and our future, topics to be addressed in future sermons. This morning we will stick to the PAST.

Paul had once persecuted "the followers of the way" thinking they were the "wrong way." Suddenly he saw that those he persecuted were inextricably connected with the ancient *faith* of Israel. He came to understand God's new covenant as inseparable from God's old covenant. When Paul acknowledged that the God in Moses and the God in the prophets and the God in Jesus was one and the same God, that *"truth of faith"* became the basis for his becoming a Christian. That is exactly what each generation and certainly ours has to discover and do for ourselves. The God of generations past can be ours only *VIA* our acceptance.

Remember how the Gospel according to John opened? "In the beginning was the Way or the Word"—the Greek *logos* makes no difference—"and the way or the word was with God and the way or the word was God, ...and that way became evident in history, by becoming one of us, full of grace and *truth*." *(1:1ff.)* Thereafter, we must take up the story ourselves, we must carry on the story and the tradition by acknowledging that God's purposes have become our purposes and that to the best of our abilities, we will try to live according to those purposes in our lives.

Perhaps it is unnecessary to point all this out—but I will anyhow—that all this spiritual-church-God business is not merely polite reflection on ancient and eternal verities that may seem trivial in the modern sense of the term. Rather religion is concerned about temporal realities, daily realities, life and death issues.

Early on in my life came the realization—from where it came I don't really know—that God was related to real life and especially life-together, that the spiritual reality of the presence of God pertains to real life here and now, yours and mine, ours and others, not removed and unrelated, but that which brings meaning and value and vitality and helps us make sense of our existence.

* * * * *

I have been intrigued by the correlation of two Scriptural passages for some time now, one from John (14:6) and the other from Paul (I Corinthians 13:13). At the center of Christian life is **"THE ENCOMPASSING CROSS"** that not only stands at the center of history, but at the center of our experience encompassing our lives. This *"truth of faith"* becomes clearer when we stretch out these ideas in time. For, ultimately, our human dilemma is a temporal dilemma, a problem of time. Time is our ultimate scarcity. Theology is basically our reflection on God and time as we experience both in passing. We experience the presence of God in terms of past, present and future. The little diagram that serves as our frontpiece and this little sermon may seem so simple as to be simple-minded, but it represents how I came to understand God as revealed in the Bible and in human experience. And I hope it might prove beneficial for others. The columns also illustrate the relationship of some key concepts that are frequently not very clearly understood. They, too, are all centered in **"THE ENCOMPASSING CROSS"** of Christ.

Our wrestling match with the passage of time is not merely a matter of how fast time flies, or in some cases how slow it goes, nor our acknowledging painfully the aging process, nor how a certain man past fifty can no longer dunk a basketball or even dream about it anymore. Rather our wrestling match with God and the passage of time pertains to what it means to live and work, relate and cooperate, what it means both to be and not to be and what it means to spend time…what it means to ask ourselves right now, "What time is it—really—for any of us— right now?"

* * * * *

The Bible and the doctrines and dogmas of Christian theology are basically human struggles with life and meaning in terms of time. Ideas such as the Trinity deal with matters of time and history. They are designed to help us better understand how God is present in our history—how God is present in our experience—how God is with us in our time.

For example, the TRINITY, meaning *tri*-ad, essential threeness or being threefold, or *tri*-une or, better yet, *tri*-unity—this idea of God as oneness in threeness is an attempt to answer the question, how can the one God of the universe and all of creation become a human being and dwell among us in history, even die and, though we claim, resurrected, still be a present reality with us today 2000 years later—as vital today as when Jesus walked and talked with Thomas and His disciples around the sea of Galilee? The Trinity attempts to answer that question. The Trinity demonstrates how God is related to both creation and history, past and present and future—a matter of time and the passage of time, but with emphasis on the presence of God throughout time. Most important for the church (and for you and me) is that our trinitarian belief provides us with the assurance that God is present with us today as God was present with us yesterday as God will be with us tomorrow and forever. That's the all-important Trinity or Tri-unity temporal point, the eternal presence of God throughout the passage of time. This morning I want to point out that there are different and distinct terms that help us understand that passage.

Our best example is the CROSS OF CHRIST, which helps us understand the presence of God and the passage of our time— even while it transcends time and stands over the wrecks of time (some wrecks with which we are personally all too familiar). Jesus Christ remains at the center of the cross and the crossroads of time. So look once again at that diagram that serves as our frontpiece. THE ENCOMPASSING CROSS—constitutes a *temporal formula and spiritual template* (templet) that helps us make sense of our passing, our spiritual experience.

Consider each word of Jesus' statement,

"I AM the way, the truth and the life." (14: 6)[7]

1. For the Christian the essential *Truth*—as has been suggested—is past, centered in the historical cross of Christ.
2. *Life* is right now in the present.
3. And the *Way* always lies ahead of us.

Here is a spiritual framework that stretches life out temporally extending it backwards and forwards while experiencing its passage in each passing-present moment.

When we correlate this Johannine verse with that famous Pauline line,

"So faith, hope, love abide these three, but the greatest of these is love."(I Corinthians 13:13)

we can see and appreciate how *FAITH AND TRUTH* belong together. They are both Christ-centered and rooted in a past event, the formative event for Christians. Again, the historical reality of Jesus Christ is the basis of Christian *truth* claims and the starting point of Christian *faith*. The Christ-Event happened and because it happened—a past reality—everything present and everything future is transformed.

That past Christ-Event provides our historical foundation for projecting a Future and our *Hope* in it, for *Hope* is always Future even as is our *Way* stretching out ever before us. The Future is God's and, consequently, that too is a great source of confidence. Our Way is always *Hope*-filled. I might add that many people fail to distinguish between faith and hope, and tend to use these terms almost as if they are synonyms, but

15

they refer to different temporal realities and different aspects of our spiritual, human experience. Faith is past; Hope is future.

And, thirdly, there is that final and all important dimension which is right now, the present moment, where *life* and *love* are interrelated in everything we do and say as Christians. Right now is where past and future meet.

Jesus Christ at the center of the Cross and the Center of all our Crossroads. *TRI-VIA*, indeed, that informs and influences and inspires. Thanks be unto God.

I thank You God for most this amazing
day: for the leaping greenly spirits of trees
and a blue true dream of sky: and for everything
which is natural which is infinite which is yes

(i who have died and am alive again today,
and this is the sun's birthday; this is the birth
day of life and love and wings: and of gay
great happening illimitably earth)

how should tasting touching hearing seeing
breathing any-lifted from the no
of all nothing-human merely being
doubt unimaginable you.

(now the ears of my ears awake and
now the eyes of my eyes are opened)

* * * * *

We can never be born enough. We are human beings, for whom birth is a supremely welcome mystery, the mystery of growing: the mystery which happens only and whenever we are faithful to ourselves. You and I wear the dangerous looseness of doom and find it becoming...Miracles are to come. With you I leave a remembrance of miracles: they are by somebody who can love and who shall be continually reborn....[1]

18

FIRST HAND FAITH

In the words of e e cummings, "We can never be born enough." But as Nicodemus once asked, "How can this be?" (John 3:9) The answer is not physical; we're talking about spiritual miracles—new beginnings, new insights, multiple transformations of the soul attune for the first time to realities previously unknown and even unimagined. Lives changed—of people previously thought unchangeable and beyond hope. Such are the mysteries of what can be called, *FIRST-HAND FAITH*, the result of being ever open to the Spirit of God alive and at work in history and human life.

"We can never be born enough" *spiritually*.

Like so many other spiritual realities, the idea of being "born-again" has been variously defined and claimed by one group or another as their exclusive property, so that many of us cringe at the thought of having to answer someone accosting us on a street corner with *the question*,

"Are you a 'born-again' Christian?"

Whatever happened to the old, equally obnoxious question,

"Are you saved?"

Such questions can obscure and misconstrue the miraculous beauty and mysterious power of *FIR8T-HAND FAITH*, the realization that "we can never be born enough."

* * * * *

This sermon was delivered on Mother's Day, May 9, 1993. The message is appropriate for Lenten reflection or confirmation or the reception of new members or for encouraging people to take that first great step of faith based on their own experience. The Gospel and Epistle lessons were taken from John 3:1-9; I John 5:4, Acts 9:1-9 and Romans 1:8-17.

I have been intrigued for some time now by accounts of *first-hand religious experiences* or direct confrontations with God, intimate-immediate contacts with the living Lord. Such encounters result in the transformation of human lives. The old is suddenly made new. One long thought lost forever is found. Life is literally turned completely around—
like the Apostle Paul
and Saint Augustine
and Martin Luther
and John Wesley
and numerous others we have known personally.

All four of these reformers exemplify—they epitomize for us—
FIR8T-HAND FAITH. They represent what many mothers have known throughout the centuries and lived quietly accordingly.

All four men had dramatic conversion experiences that changed their lives as many women discovered dramatically too when they became mothers. Mothers know how biological birth and being spiritually born again can come in one action-packed event.

All four men also were steeped in *second-hand faith,* that is, they had heard the stories, the traditions, and learned from the examples of their parents and other cultural influences, having inherited the collective wisdom of their ancestors. These men were products of their respective times and places and reflected for the most part the attitudes and thoughts—whether positively or negatively—of their fore-fathers and fore-mothers.

Their respective "conversions" were literally dramatic "turning points" which enabled them to serve with confidence and courage, and live sacrificially and unconditionally thereafter. Because they had *experienced first-hand the love of the Lord in their lives.*

But their new spiritual points of departure cannot be seen apart from their previous religious training that had prepared them for accepting *FAITH FIR8T-HAND* and saying "YES!" to God!

They may have acknowledged God's existence before, but without any great excitement—tacit acknowledgement at best, but without any real enthusiasm.

Then in each case a unique configuration of circumstances and events occurred which changed their lives. They were born-again. They then knew personally what they had previously only acknowledged as a possibility, perhaps even a slim and unlikely possibility. Or, we might say, where once they had been academically acquainted, now they were existentially assured. Their intellectual hesitancy had been turned into spiritual certainty. They felt God's presence where before they could only talk about it on the basis of someone else's experience, something they had read about or heard about. God's call had been confirmed in their own experience, when they affirmed God's presence in their lives.

Job had once asked,

"Oh, that I knew where I might find God." (23:3)

Later he found the God he had been seeking and could say,

"I had heard of thee by the hearing of the ear, but now my eye sees thee;..." (42:5)[2]

* * * * *

Consider with me for a few minutes each of our four reformers, men who radically transformed the world. Saul's dramatic Damascus road, 360 degree turnabout is, of course, the classic example of what is called a conversion or born-again experience. He excelled in his second-hand training. He wrote how he had been "circumcised on the eighth day" in the best of his religious tradition, "of the tribe of Benjamin, a Hebrew born of Hebrews; (and) as to the law a Pharisee. (Philippians 3:5) Why, he had even studied under the great Professor Gamaliel, etc. He was credentialed.

In Saul's case, due to fervent loyalty to Hebraic tradition, he had opposed the God of these strange new "people of the

Way." He had even stood at the periphery of a mob and witnessed—if not participated in—the first Christian martyrdom. Maybe he had actually cast a stone at Stephen? But you can be sure he heard Stephen's testimony and listened as Stephen told his faith-story to his executioners. There is no question in my mind that Saul was radically affected by what he had seen and heard and perhaps done. How much of his conversion was due to his background experiences plus a conscience working overtime on his mind and heart? And how much was God involved in stirring up Saul's mental and emotional situation? We don't know, nor do we need to know. But we do know Saul was literally born again. He heard God asking him, "Saul, Saul, why do you persecute me?" The profound metaphor of "once being blind, but now I see" suddenly took on new meaning for him. Saul was born again as Paul—an act of **FIRST-HAND FAITH**, a new man emerged as if from a concrete cocoon. Once he had been a bystander at best, a persecutor at worst. Thereafter he would live at the epicenter of Christian Faith. For it would be Paul's interpretation of Christian faith more than any other that transformed the world. It was Paul who wrote that portion of the Epistle to the Romans that is our text this morning, a most influential passage that has transformed so many lives throughout the centuries.

* * * * *

A few hundred years later, our second reformer, St. Augustine (354-430) was tremendously influenced by this same Letter of Paul to the Romans and his conversion can be attributed in large measure to Pauline Christianity.[3] St. Augustine was also well-schooled in both philosophy and theology. It wasn't the Letter to the Romans alone or any philosophical tradition that changed his life; it was the reality of the Spirit of God at work in and through his mother and other influences that accounts for his transformation—like Paul before him. It was largely Augustine's influence that held the Christian Church together, following the fall of the Roman Empire.

* * * * *

Without dwelling on this second example it was in this Augustinian tradition, much later that a man named Martin Luther (1483-1546) emerged. He entered an Augustinian monastery and received most of his religious training there. He agonized with what he had inherited second-hand, both from St. Paul and St. Augustine and others, until in his own first-hand experience he came to know for himself the love and forgiveness and acceptance of God. And it happened while reading—as you might have imagined—Romans 1:17. It was then that the realization came upon Luther suddenly that it was faith alone (sola fidei) that mattered, and that faith was a gift of God, a gracious gift that cannot be earned, but given freely.[4] In receiving it, believing it, basing our lives on it, God's grace alone (sola gratia) is experienced. Again, remember all three of these men were well-trained and highly educated, schooled in the best that Christian faith second-hand had to offer them.

St Paul's Letter to the Romans runs like a red thread through our common history and heritage. Each of these three men had to have the love of God they read about confirmed in their own experience. We can be led to the love of God by means of reading Romans or by being reared in our respective religious traditions—like being led to water like a horse—but we have to receive the spiritual reality of Christ for ourselves. *No one can believe for another*. Moreover, it's not that these men had not been good and faithful to the best of their abilities prior to their being born-again. But their *FIRST-HAND FAITH EXPERIENCES*—their personal acceptance of God's love—would constitute thereafter their starting over and turning around and beginning again. In their own intimate and immediate experience their second-hand faith had been confirmed by their first hand affirmation.

Had Paul and Augustine and Luther discovered God or had God discovered them? What is the combination or mixture of divine and human ingredients that creates a conversion or spiritual transformation? I do not want to detract from the importance of a personal affirmation and direct contact with God *first-hand.* Because without that experience, our Christian faith is incomplete. However, we don't know how much of any so-called "born-again" experience is due to a divine thunderbolt suddenly intervening and interrupting life and how much is actually due to the steady, plodding influence of our own upbringing and training. This curious combination of divine and human elements that initiates our faith will always remain a spiritual mystery. But I am sure that many spiritual mid-wives are involved in all our spiritual births.

How many spiritual births are due to a persistent parent having planted a seed that finally sprouted and blossomed, perhaps following a long adolescent drought?

How much may be due to a patient teacher whose lesson plans finally paid off, or a sermon heard, or a devotion read or a prayer?

How much may be due to the affirming and encouraging influence of a significant other or a good friend who wouldn't give up on us?

My guess is that all this was operative in Paul and Augustine and Luther's situations. In addition they had reached the limits of their quests for understanding and meaning. Finally, they released themselves to God and to their utter amazement they found that God sustained them.

Like these three men, we too live by *FAITH FIRST-HAND,* whereas previously we only knew what we heard second-hand. Wherever and whenever our understanding stops, our respective searches end, our limits reached, there our faith really begins. It begins by believing, accepting God's acceptance of us, by our saying "YES!" to God's love in Christ. That's as close as I can come in trying to understand what it means to be born-again or converted or as I prefer, experiencing *FAITH FIRST-HAND!* It begins in surrender and decision and acceptance....

* * * * *

There is no better example than our fourth reformer, John Wesley (1703-1791), a product of an Anglican rectory and

24

reared in the Christian faith. At Governor Oglethorpe's invitation, he had come to Georgia as a young man intent on converting the Indians.

In reflecting on that experience later, Wesley wrote,

"I went to America to convert the Indians; but O who shall convert me? Who, what, is he that will deliver me from this *evil heart of unbelief*?

I have a fair summer religion," he continued—Don't we all?— "I can talk well; nay, and believe myself while no danger is near; but let death look me in the face and my spirit is troubled….(1/24/1738)

"…what have I learned…? Why, what I least of all expected, that I, who went to America to convert others, was never myself converted to God."

Wesley returned to England (2/29/1738) engaged in the birth pains of spiritual struggle, immersed in intellectual confusion and academic turmoil and filled with intense personal dissatisfaction. He felt his faith was still second-hand and not confirmed first-hand as it was for his Moravian friends who were at peace with themselves and assured of God's presence. God was not fully real to Wesley yet. He was not sure of Christ and he was not at spiritual peace within himself. He knew what he wanted, but he hadn't attained it.

"The faith I want," he said, "is a sure trust and confidence in God that through the merits of Christ my sins are forgiven."

(Or, we might say that "things between God and us are alright")

On another occasion he wrote,

"I want that faith which none can have without knowing that he hath it,…having peace with God through Christ."

All this sounds a lot like Luther's intense struggle or reminiscent of Augustine's agony in his *Confessions* or Paul's confession outlined in the seventh chapter of Romans. There is an almost morbid introspection evident in these men, their sense of sin and the great gap between what they felt they should be, but couldn't be and weren't.

Then a few months later the *locus classicus* in the annals of Methodism occurred. Wesley wrote in his *Journal* on May 24th,

"In the evening I went very unwillingly to a society in Aldersgate Street where one was reading Luther's preface to the Epistle to the Romans. About a quarter before nine, while he was describing the change which God works in the heart through faith in Christ, I felt my heart strangely warmed. I felt I did trust in Christ, Christ alone for my salvation: and an assurance was given me that he had taken away my sins, even mine, and saved me from the law of sin and death...I then testified openly to all there what I...felt in my heart."[5]

Peace had come, assurance had been given, love received, a human heart strangely warmed and there emerged a "born-again" Christian. Wesley's life was now confirmed in Christ and transformed as a consequence. He described his new found faith as follows:

"I *now* believe the Gospel is true. I 'show my faith by my works,' by staking my all upon it. I would do so again and again a thousand times, if the choice were (mine) still to make. Whoever sees me sees I would be a Christian...."[6]

"Faith is a work of God in us which transforms us and makes us to be born again of God, and put to death the old man in us and makes of us entirely new men in heart, courage, thought and all our powers."[7]

I find it amazing that Luther had learned this from the Epistle to the Romans, from Paul and Augustine and now Wesley learned it from Luther—all these world-renowned reformers of Christianity knew Christ in their hearts by faith first hand and the twin *truth* that—to quote more from that same Epistle—the Spirit

> "bears witness with our spirit, that we are (all) children of God." (8:16)

After the Aldersgate meeting John hurried home to share the good news with his brother Charles. In Charles Wesley's *Journal* that night there appears the following entry:

"Toward ten o'clock my brother was brought in triumph by a troop of our friends, and declared, 'I believe!'" The diary adds, "We sang a hymn with great joy and parted with prayer."

Before we sing a hymn with great joy and part with prayer, we should linger a few more minutes on the transforming power of God's love that can change as Wesley said, "his evil heart of unbelief" into a "heart strangely warmed." *BECAUSE THAT IS WHAT PARENTS AND THE CHURCH ARE FOR*, with unfair emphasis this morning on mothers. Because it is primarily mothers who nurture the spiritual soil in their children by telling them stories and passing on the traditions that provide the environment conducive for a child to accept for himself or herself the *truth* of what they have heard, what they have been told and taught. *FIRST-HAND FAITH* does not ride on a lightening bolt and enter an unprepared mind or unwarmed heart. If our children don't receive solid second-hand training at home or in their church, chances are they're not going to have a *FIRST-HAND FAITH*, for they won't be told of *the truths of faith* elsewhere. The foundation has to be established; the groundwork is so important. And mothers are the primary transmitters of attitudes and values and second-hand faith that create a receptive child.

Even more significant is the role mothers play in inspiring *FIRST-HAND FAITH*. They provide examples for their children that awaken their spirits. Mothers are not only primary transmitters of the truths of second-hand faith, they are the primary transformers of *FAITH FIRST-HAND. BECAUSE IT IS IN THE EXPERIENCE OF BEING LOVED, KNOWING YOU ARE LOVED, BEING ACCEPTED AND APPRECIATED UNCONDITIONALLY THAT WE EXPERIENCE FIRST-HAND FAITH IN GOD*. That experience does not come exclusively from mothers. It can come from fathers, friends, siblings, significant

27

others, even strangers, but primarily from mothers. Examples of trust and self-sacrifice and forgiveness demonstrate the love of God in Christ and lead us to affirm for ourselves that love.

On the Sunday following his Aldersgate experience Wesley took as his sermon text I John, chapter 5, verse 4, a fitting conclusion for us this morning.

> "For whatever is born of God overcomes the world.
> And this is the victory that overcomes the world, our
> . faith."

Indeed it is faith in the love of God alive within us, among us, from our biological births and through all our spiritual rebirths, that sustain and give us hope.

While we can all be grateful for the *FIRST-HAND FAITH* of our world changing reformers, greater gratitude is due our world transformers, our mothers, whose faith and hope and love ever nourishes and inspires. For most of what the world knows of faith and hope and love has come to us either from our mothers or others who assume that role.

Thanks be unto God for the Apostle Paul, Saint Augustine, Martin Luther, John Wesley and many others, but especially our mothers, through Jesus Christ our Lord, Amen.

Oh God of earth and air and fire,
Our joyful hearts lift up, inspire!
Ignite a warmth within our breast,
And light our minds with wisdom's best.

Illumine us, celestial fire.
To see and do what you require:
Be just to all in ev'ry place,
Be kind to all the human race.

Rekindle Pentecostal fire:
True eloquence may we acquire;
Touch ev'ry tongue with truth aflame,
That we with skill your love proclaim.

You led your fold with cloud and fire:
Our Guide is One whom we admire;
You're there to lead at ev'ry turn,
And we press on with hearts that burn.[1]

ON FIRE INSIDE

At an annual meeting of a child care association convened in Sacramento, California, a number of years ago, the speaker was berating the audience of child care workers about the high rate of burn-out among those who work with abused and abandoned children. With obvious reference to three nuns sitting in the front row, he asked the audience, "Aside from the fact that some of you just happen to be nuns, what are we going to do to stop burn-out in our profession?"

I started to laugh inside, because he had already answered his own question but didn't realize it. Those nuns just didn't happen to be nuns, it was precisely their *faith*, their commitment, their decision and the presence of God they sensed within them, that sustained them, that kept them from burning-out and that enabled them to continue when others quit. They were "On Fire Inside!" Their enthusiasm—literally—made the difference as the word *enthusiasm*, from the Greek *en/theos*, means "in God" or "God in us." It's the flames of such enthusiasm or the fires of faith, or hearts on fire, or John Wesley's "burning hearts," that is the answer to any form of "burn-out...."

The speaker could have equally said, "Aside from the fact that some of you just happen to be Christians,..." Because I'm sure there were other Christians there too. It's just harder to recog-

---

This sermon was delivered November 25, 1990 with text taken from Jeremiah 20:7-12 and Luke 24:13-19, 25-32. An earlier version based on the same theme was presented during Lent in 1976.

The idea for this sermon came from W. Sherman Skinner (1906-1976) who served as the Synod Executive of the Synod of Southern California while I was serving as Senior Pastor of the Upland Presbyterian Church. His sermon entitled "Fire in His Bones" was reprinted in the *Princeton Seminary Bulletin* LVIII, Number 1, October, 1964, pp. 36-40.

nize a Christian these days. Perhaps we need name tags to identify us? Because unlike nuns, we're not known by the 'habits' we wear. But wouldn't it be great if we were recognized by our *living habits*, by our sparkling attitudes, by our treatment of others, by our good deeds? Wouldn't it be great to hear people say, "There goes a member of First Federated Church, I can tell, because they are the ones with 'hearts on fire;' they never burn-out. Those federated folk are on fire inside. And their lives show it."

Emil Brunner, a noted 20th century Protestant theologian, once stated, "The church exists for mission as fire exists for burning."[2] Wouldn't it be great if we would be recognized by what we do, by our mission, for where there is no mission, there is no church. Where there is no fire inside, there is no mission outside. We need to keep before us constantly the need to rekindle those spiritual fires inside, and to stoke those mission embers lest our own fires of faith be extinguished and we become burnt out inside and outside.

We want to keep our spiritual fires burning or, if necessary, even rediscover those fires once again. It may seem strange, given that goal, to use Jeremiah as our starting point, though he is a favorite prophetic personality who intrigues me. To the popular imagination he probably represents not a bright light, but a dim bulb.

John Henry (Cardinal) Newman (1801-1890) once wrote,
> "Lead, kindly LIght, amid the encircling gloom
> Lead Thou me on; The night is dark, and I am far from home;
> Lead Thou me on;
> Keep Thou my feet; I do not ask to see the distance scene—
> One step enough for me."

It is such a powerful hymn, an expression of a patient pilgrim plodding through the dark night of a lifetime surrounded by danger and impending disaster with every step taken, but remaining ever confident that God is ever present and always leading us onward and upward. I'm reminded of Albrecht

Dürer's (1471-1528) engraving, entitled "Knight Devil and Death." So Newman's hymn suggests strength and courage, perseverance and confidence, despite all earthly evidence to the contrary...

Jeremiah was no Albrecht Dürer. Jeremiah was no John Henry Newman. There was little "kindly light" in this prophet. In fact, a whole lot more darkness than light. I don't know how familiar you are with Mr. Gloom and Doom, so a little extra introduction might be helpful. I'm sure, that whereas both Jesus and Jeremiah's hearts were on fire inside, we are probably more familiar with the spiritual impression Jesus made on, for example, his travelling companions as they walked and talked and shared scripture together on the road to Emmaus, than we are Jeremiah's prophetic influence. Jesus touched their hearts with God's love and as John Wesley noted, "Did not we feel an unusual warmth of love!" "Was not our heart burning (within us)?"[3] But it would be a mistake to make a simple distinction between Jeremiah and justice in the Old Testament and Jesus and love in the New. Indeed, Jeremiah's fire inside burned because of his righteous indignation, that burned like an ulcer because of God's concern for justice. Nevertheless, we must remember that it was also Jeremiah whose new covenant was written on Israelite hearts, not on tablets of stone.[4] Similarly, Jesus was equally concerned about injustice and not just love. So the idea of hearts on fire inside us really combines both God's passionate quest for justice and the energy of God's love.

＊ ＊ ＊ ＊ ＊

Some people identified Jeremiah with Jesus, who once had asked his disciples, "Who do men say that the son of man is?" And they answered,

> "Some say John the Baptist, others say Elijah, and others say Jeremiah or one of the prophets!" (Matthew 16:14)

Again, wouldn't it be wonderful if someone today would confuse one of us with anything reminiscent of Jeremiah or Jesus or one of the prophets?

As a prophet Jeremiah was God's mouthpiece on earth, because that is what a prophet's job was, to proclaim God's outrageous love and denounce crimes against the helpless and oppressed. Jeremiah took his responsibility very seriously. The hand of God weighed very heavily upon him as God was almost always mad at Israel. So Jeremiah was caught between God's anger and the ever belligerent, always disobedient, Israelites. He was caught in the middle in the cross-fire.

One of his favorite phrases in Hebrew was, *magor missabib*, which meant "terror on every side." It may well have become his nickname because he used it so frequently in his prophesying.[5] We might even imagine townspeople whispering in the market place when they saw old Jeremiah coming toward them, nudging one another and saying, "Here comes old Magor Missabib," for Jeremiah seldom had anything good to say, only "terror on every side." Doom peddler and Jeremiah were almost synonyms.

Though Jeremiah didn't always like his unenviable responsibility, he carried out his prophetic call obediently and with a sense of urgency. Above all, he and God were in constant dialogue. No one had a more intimate relationship with God than Jeremiah and his living habits and life style demonstrated his deep and abiding personal and spiritual relationship with God. Jeremiah's various broodings about their mutually shared misery, their commiseration, if you will, were written down. They are called his "Confessions" and can be found throughout the book that bears his name.[6] They read like the intensely personal problems of the psalmist or the woes of Job, but in Jeremiah's case there is even an English word named after his laments; a *Jeremiad* means a complaint, or a tale of woe.[7]

Over the years Jeremiah's confessions became increasingly hostile and in the end they read more like Hamlet's soliloquies than dialogues with God, for as far as Jeremiah was concerned, God no longer answered him or talked with him or paid any attention to him. Jeremiah felt that not only had he been mis used and abused, but that God had tricked him, even "deceived" him, the very word used for a young man who seduced or enticed a maiden.[8] He exploded angrily using the seductive metaphor. "God, you seized me, you forced me, for you were stronger than me. Now everyone laughs at me. It makes me sick inside. I'm a joke...."

Earlier in the sixth chapter he had complained,

> "I'm filled with the wrath of the Lord; I am weary of holding it in." (6:11)

And later in the 15th chapter he similarly complained,

> "I did not sit in the company of merrymakers, nor did I rejoice; I sat alone, because thy hand was upon me, for thou hadst filled me with indignation." (15:7)

Jeremiah had been batted about, collared and locked up in stocks and scorned by the public, but the text we read this morning from the 20th chapter describes his most bitter, bleakest hour, the dark night of his soul. He was on the verge of burn-out, but he found he couldn't even do that. His outburst bordered on blasphemy, because he had had it with God. Like Johnny Paycheck's old song, he wanted to tell God, "Take this job and shove it." He wanted to call it quits forever, but couldn't.

In addition to all his problems, there was this pipsqueak of a temple policeman (pipsqueak might be Hebrew for wimp), a court priest, the kind that keep you on hold forever when you call government offices in Washington. In Jeremiah's case the ecclesiastical bureaucrat was named Pashur. Pashur not only always opposed Jeremiah, but was responsible for his punishment and imprisonment. Pashur could have been the final irritation, Jeremiah's last straw, because Pashur apparently preached happiness and prosperity—what the people wanted to hear, not what God wanted to tell them. That makes Pashur a 'false prophet,' but who cared? The people liked him. Pashur made them feel secure, whether they should feel secure or not. You know, no problem, no deficit, no taxes, no shortages, no war…, nothing to worry about, like Bobby McFerrin's more recent song, "Don't Worry—Be Happy!" Pashur declared no harm would befall them. He probably also proclaimed, "Peace, Peace," which really irritated Jeremiah, who believed,

> "There would be no peace." (6:14; 8:11)

Jeremiah probably could have endured the persecution along with the pain of imprisonment. He probably could have endured even the humiliation of Pashur and the rejection of the people, but he couldn't continue as one who felt deceived and abandoned by God. And that's exactly how he felt…ABANDONED BY GOD!

I don't know if any of you have ever felt that way? Ignored by God, cheated, deceived, unfairly treated, persecuted for doing your job, imprisoned for your faithfulness! I'm not talking about not being appreciated for your services or acknowledged adequately for your contributions or efforts. I'm talking about a deeper sense of rejection, personal violation.

Now all this is still a preface to our text, which provides psychoanalytic insight into prophetic consciousness and Jeremiah's intense spiritual struggle with God. Jeremiah wanted out; but couldn't get out. Though he was infuriated and unleashed his fury against God in one of prophetic literature's most impressive passages, still he wasn't burned-out; because God still had a hold of his heart, which is precisely what made Jeremiah so furious. You can't burn-out, if God's fire is inside. We can almost hear him crying out,

> "Even when I try to forget you, Lord…
>
> Even when I tell myself I'll never prophesy or mention your name again, there is in my heart as it were a burning fire (inside), shut up in my bones, and I am weary with holding it in, and I cannot." (20:9)

What a tremendous passage with such a profound spiritual insight into the struggle of the human soul. Yes, that is *SOUL!* What God puts inside us is *SOUL.*

Though infuriated, Jeremiah's heart or soul was still on fire...
Though deeply disturbed and a whirlwind of rage inside, he
was still very much alive spiritually...

Though he felt a tightening deep inside, as he said, like a fire
locked up in his chest, which he couldn't contain, no matter
how hard he tried, he knew the fire inside was divinely ignited.
God had put it there just as God had placed the burning coal in
the prophet Isaiah's mouth.[9] Deep within was a mysteriously
irresistible inner compulsion, an "inner necessity," which constitutes our Christian calling, our vocation, what God wants us
to be and do. The ever-tenacious God wouldn't let go of
Jeremiah. He had a heart-hold on him. Similarly, the fire God
starts inside us is a dynamic, driving force—fueled by soul-
power—because it is God at work within us.

*　*　*　*　*

Is there anything like this going on inside us?

Is God in any way our driving force inside? If so, where are we
being driven? Is there anything we are literally *enthusiastic*
about today? Do we have anything going on in our lives with
which we can identify Christian vocation, or God's calling, or
any God-given "inner necessity"? Or, is all this so much religious gobbledygook? Are these spiritual experiences reserved
exclusively for ancient prophets like Jeremiah or Isaiah, or
apostles like Paul or men like Cleopas on the road to Emmaus?
Does this make any sense? It should speak to our soul, because
if it doesn't, we're wasting our time and God's; for we're spiritually dead; the fire once inside has gone out.

Fortunately, that's not the case. The metaphor of hearts on fire
inside and enthusiastic souls is as relevant and vital now as
ever, if we believe God is at work in the world, in the church,
and in us. The divinely ignited fire inside us was placed within
us by God's grace for a purpose and is as powerful a com-
pelling force today as ever before. The biblical examples of
Jeremiah and Jesus provide us with clues as to why God puts
fire inside us, why God gives us souls:

37

First, that we might feel the same righteous indignation or divine discontent that God feels regarding this world and its iniquities and its inequities.

And, secondly, that we might feel the same outrageous love God feels for humanity. Despite our persistent human indifference to one another, God works within us. We are the only instruments or agents available to accomplish God's purposes among us. This is an astoundingly inefficient method of operating; but, nevertheless, God's chosen modus operandi.

It is, of course, God's mission that accounts for God's spirit being placed within us. That's why we are on fire inside. God is stirring us up, inspiring us to serve, to fulfill God's mission on this *globe*.

Now I know where I'm going and, I think, where we need to be going and what we need to be asking ourselves in the future. What is God's mission today? What's going on on this globe that really bothers God today? Because if there is any fire inside us that God ignited....(and it's not to be confused with schizophrenia or dementia or the onset of a coronary, the after-effects of overeating, an ulcer or the flu, nor misconstrued as an emotional breakdown, mid-life crisis, or the ever popular, burn-out...) If there is any fire inside us that God ignited, it has to do with our God-given global mission.

Unfortunately, but frequently, God's mission and preoccupation with love and justice issues have been reduced to our individual responsibilities in relation to what we do with what we have and how we relate to one another at the shopping mall. I submit to you that such a simple approach to our God-given mission misses the mission and trivializes the message. And, I don't want to diminish in any way the importance of our personal responsibility and our interpersonal relationships. I, too, get upset if a healthy teenager takes the designated handicapped parking place, etc. But God's mission is more than personal relationships and thanksgiving baskets once a year. Moreover, God's concerns must be more global and not restricted to local or regional or even cultural concerns. I believe there are at least four global areas of life about which God is very much concerned, if not mad about these days and, consequently, four valid reasons why we should be on fire inside. I mention all four without embellishment or explanation and without any discussion of their important social and political context or implications. Nor are they arranged in any priority:

1. nuclear reality globally is a definite concern,
2. population explosion with astounding global consequences,
3. the many faces of poverty worldwide,
4. and the global destruction of the environment.

I'm not trying to delimit God's concerns to these four.

What would you add or delete? What do you think is important to God, and consequently, what do we believe God wants for us and from us? Remember, God is in us to make us just as disturbed by injustice and just as energized by love as God is!

So may God upset us and deeply disturb us.

May God set us on fire inside and spiritually excite us to participate in God's global mission.

May God grab our hearts and hold on when our global frustrations get the best of us and we want to quit.

We pray, O God, that you not let go of us nor give up on us, nor our globe, but fan those flames of mission latent within us, so that we might fulfill the mission you have called us to accomplish. It is your divine spark, your eternal flame, your abiding spiritual presence that provides our lives with meaning and purpose, that gives us direction and keeps us going even when others around us have stopped dead in their tracks. And, finally, Gracious God, help us neither to ignore nor deny nor in any way snuff out those little fires you have started within us. Inspire and sustain us that your purposes for us and for this globe be fulfilled....

Faith According to John Calvin—

For unbelief is so deeply rooted in our hearts, and we are so inclined to it, that not without hard struggle is one able to persuade himself of what all confess with the mouth; namely, that God is Faithful. (*Institutes* III, 11 15)

For faith does not certainly promise itself either length of years or honor or riches in this life, since the Lord willed that none of these things be appointed for us. But it is content with this certainty: that however many things fail us that have to do with the maintenance of this life, God will never fail. (*Institutes* III, 11 28)

Now we shall possess a right definition of faith if we call it a firm and certain knowledge of God's Benevolence toward us, founded upon the truth of the freely given promise in Christ, both revealed to our minds and sealed upon our hearts through the Holy Spirit. (*Institutes* III, 11 7)

LEAPING FORWARD
FAITHFULLY

I have done a little research on leap year and learned that an Anglo Saxon monk, named "Venerable Bede" or St. Bede (672-735), back in 730 A.D.[1] discovered that the Julien calendar (from Julius Caesar) which had been initiated in 46 B.C. was 11 minutes and 14 seconds too long each year. Time apparently ran a little faster back then. That miscalculation amounted to about one day every 128 years so that by the time of Pope Gregory XIII (1502-1585), the error had accumulated to 10 days. Pope Gregory, innovator of our modern calendar, decreed that the day after October 4, 1582, would be October 15th, thus lopping off ten days.[2]

That's temporal if not eternal power. Can you imagine how many problems that decision could have caused—and would cause, if done today? Maybe way up north in Oslo or Stockholm, where they didn't hear about these missing ten days for decades, some important document could have been signed, perhaps on what was thought to have been October 10th. Since there was no such day, was the document valid or not? The case could be in Norwegian or Swedish courts for years. Meanwhile back home in Rome, some Italian had a CD come due on the 10th? Would the bank give him his money? More than likely, most people back then didn't know what day it was anyhow, and if they did, it wouldn't make any differ-

This sermon was delivered March 1, 1992 at First Federated Church, Peoria, Illinois. Recall that 1992 was a Leap Year which provides the point of departure for the sermon. Scripture lessons were taken from Genesis 22:1-14, Hebrews 11:17-18, Luke 6:22-23, Acts 3:1-16; 14:8-23.

ence. **Survival** was the difference every day made. And for most people in our world today, the same thing could be said.

In 1752 the British government imposed this Gregorian calendar on its colonies, decreeing that the day after September 2nd, would be September 14th, a loss of 11 days. The birthdays of those before that date and still living were changed accordingly, so Washington's birthday was moved from the 11th (OS or Old Style) to the 22nd. I won't go on, though I am intrigued by the mysteries of Leap Year and our calendar. But it is a marvelous illustration of how time flies literally and how some days actually disappeared long ago. The question is, of course, "Where do our days go?" Some of our days might as well have been dropped from our calendars too as many of them are pretty much wasted.

I think it was Sarah Vaughn who sang, "What a Difference a Day Makes...twenty-four little hours. What a difference a day makes and the difference is you." It's a beautiful song and it's message is equally beautiful. It suggests that a day does make a lot of difference and that "YOU" and "I" are the difference that a day makes. The difference could and should be each one of us. I know the love song wasn't addressed to some generic occupant or just anyone out there. The *you* in the love song—that made all the difference—was that very special *you* in a romantic relationship. But even recognizing that important distinction, we can still acknowledge that you and I are special too. What would *we do* if we were given a bonus day? Because that's exactly what all of us have been given this leap year, an extra day.

Most people, I'm convinced, take the extra day for granted like so many other days—just another day—and the difference is not anyone or anything in particular—just another day of mindless drift and empty drivel and lost opportunity. Nothing special!

However, for some, it may be their last day or one of the few remaining days left or a day filled with unforeseen consequence or auspicious possibility.

How do we get the best from each given-day?
How can we make the most of each God-given day?
How can we celebrate each day as a gift of God?
And make a difference by what we do in it?

* * * * *

I'm reminded of a paragraph from poet/author Carl Sandburg's (1878-1967) book *Always The Young Strangers*[3] that comes much too close to home even for those of us who should know better. Wrote Galesburg's greatest,

> "I have always enjoyed riding up front in a smoking car, in a seat back of the 'deadheads,' the railroaders going back to the home base. Their talk about each other runs free.... Once I saw a young fireman in overalls take a seat and slouch down easy and comfortable. After a while a brakeman in blue uniform came along and planted himself alongside the fireman. They didn't say anything. The train ran along. The two of them didn't even look at each other. Then the brakeman, looking straight ahead, was saying, 'Well, what do you know today?' He kept looking straight ahead till suddenly he turned and stared the fireman in the face, adding, 'For sure.' I thought it was a keen...and intelligent question, (said Sandburg.) *'What do you know today—FOR 8URE?'* I remember the answer. It came slow and honest. The fireman made it plain what he knew that day for sure: (He answered,) *'Not a damn thing!'*"

I trust that Sandburg's prose is not too strong for our Sunday sensibilities. The fireman's answer could just as well be contemporary commentary. The conversation could have occurred right here in Peoria and does daily. It's a "damning" indictment of human ignorance and irresponsibility and faithlessness, especially if the firemen claimed to be Christian. Still it remains a relevant question for us to ask ourselves, *"What do we know today, or any day—for sure?"*

Since, as I've already pointed out some of our calendar difficulties, we can't even be sure what day it is. We can't be sure what time or hour it is for us. So most people reply to the brakeman's question, by saying politely "Not much!" when "not a damn thing" would come a lot closer to the *truth*. We seldom admit it, despite the fact that we go on day after day, which includes our bonus day every four years, as if we know exactly where we're going, and what we're doing, pretending to operate with a sense of certainty about ourselves and one another, absolutely sure about our jobs and our future, when if the *truth* were only known, we really don't know what we believe or what we should be doing. And, worst of all, we don't do much about it. For the Christian *FAITH FILLS THIS VOID*. Every day for us makes a difference, every person makes a difference, they are God-given gifts and God-given opportunities even though we don't know why. These are *"truths of faith."*

Now as a man of reason with a certain philosophical bent, I believe—as I have shared with you before—that "everything simultaneously makes all the difference in the world and yet no difference whatsoever." That is obviously a contradiction that verges on cynicism. But it can be and is for me the beginning of *FAITH*, that which enables me to honestly find myself living in the midst of an apparent contradiction and still believe that it minimally must make sense to someone and that someone is God.

FAITH in New Testament times didn't seem to be nearly as complicated and confusing as it is for us today. The Greek word for faith *pistis* variously meant trustworthiness, reliability, fidelity. *Pistis* was centered on the **object** of belief as well as the act of believing or the **subject**. Whenever *pistis* is translated "faith" or "trust" in the New Testament, it is taken for granted that the **object** is always worthy of that faith or trust. That's very important and can't be overemphasized. Emphasis must always be on the trustworthiness of the object of faith or GOD. God can be trusted; God can be counted on; God is always faithful!

As for the *subject* or you or me, it is not that we're unimportant, but we are secondary. We don't have to know all the right

44

answers to life's dilemmas and contradictions. But we do have to *RISK FAITH IN GOD AS TRUTH*. And that involves, *LETTING GO AND TRUSTING GOD*.

So rather than choosing to become a thorough-going cynic, I have chosen to take what Søren Kierkegaard (1813-1855) called *A LEAP OF FAITH!*[4] This is the only practical answer, which is an appropriate Christian response to the brakeman's question, "What do you know today for sure?" "God can be trusted!" Not the quality of our faith, but of God's faithfulness. Not our right answers, but God's reliability. *THE TRUTH OF FAITH IS NOT WHAT WE KNOW, BUT WHO WE KNOW AND TRUST!*

It was the story of Abraham and Isaac that we read this morning that prompted Søren Kierkegaard, the Danish Lutheran and a founder of existentialism, to suggest that in the midst of life's uncertainty and mystery, conflict and contradiction, when our questions exceed our answers—and in the midst of our deepest despair, it is necessary for us to take what he called, *"A LEAP OF FAITH!"* like a leap into the dark, a jump off the deep end, or a bungee jump from a high bridge. But it's the most important *DECISION* the Christian ever makes; for it means accepting the reality of God's love in Jesus Christ as the ultimate answer and meaning to the mysteries of human life. Not that we can ever fully understand how or why. Rather *FAITH* is our starting point, our point of reference, even our point of departure. *FAITH* begins precisely and necessarily where our understanding has reached its limits. Thereafter, it is *FAITH* that sustains us when we do not understand and cannot understand.

The classic example of Old Testament faith was Abraham, the father of all Israel, whose future depended on a son through whom descendants could be numbered, a nation formed and all people blessed. Finally, in Abraham and Sarah's old age, long after all biological prospects of birth had passed, Isaac, the promised son was born.

But then came the apparent contradiction that makes no sense whatsoever—except it shows us tremendous insight into the mysteries and complexities of human life. God asked Abraham to sacrifice his only son, Isaac, the very child God had promised. What was God doing? This is sheer madness. Crazy! Human sacrifice was so antithetical to Biblical understanding, not to mention the bizarre conditions of this particularly obnoxious test God gave Abraham? Israelite history depended on this lad, and now he was to be offered as some stupid human sacrifice.

Abraham's undaunted faith enabled him to make the necessary arrangements. The conflict must have been intensified by the boy's innocent questions, but even the boy on the altar trusted his father. And through the whole ordeal, as Abraham proceeded to prepare the sacrifice, his faith or trust in God persisted, even in the midst of what had to be a father's darkest, most desperate hour. Abraham had to experience some doubt and despair. I can't imagine any human being—even an Abraham—so absolutely sure? The author of Genesis referred to "the fear of God," but that fear, remember, included— as the text pointed out in verses 8 and 14—the trust and confidence that "the Lord would provide"[5] And that, of course is what the story is all about: God's trustworthiness and Abraham's trust.

Martin Luther's wife was troubled by this episode and is said to have asked her husband, "How could God ask Abraham to sacrifice his only son?" Martin Luther pointed out that though Isaac was spared, God gave his only son in similar sacrificial circumstances. Isn't that precisely what is seen in the encompassing Cross of Christ, the central symbol of our faith, which exceeds—again—our understanding? How can the love of God be demonstrated by a death on a cross? And yet that is what we mean by God's trustworthiness. Consider the conflict and the contradiction! And how can we be *absolutely sure* that the historical Jesus was and is and always will be the Christ of *FAITH* we claim based on that Cross? We can't! That's what THE *TRUTH OF FAITH* involves! The basis of our Christian certainty, what we know today *FOR SURE*, is that *WE CAN ALWAYS COUNT ON GOD!*

It occurred to me that the best use of our extra day this leap year would be to make sure that we used it to *"LEAP FOR-WARD FAITHFULLY"* so that every one of us might know for sure that God is *trustworthy*; therefore, we can trust the love of God beyond the mysteries and uncertainties of life and death, joy and suffering, good and evil, and regardless of our every earthly circumstance. *THE TRUTH OF FAITH IS THE CHRISTIAN ANSWER TO DESPAIR AND FUTILITY.*

To use a phrase from William James (1842-1910), it is really Christian faith...that enables us to *"LAUNCH OURSELVES IN A MOMENT OF DESPAIR,"*[6] to take that all important leap of faith, to take control by deciding for ourselves. Elsewhere this great American pragmatist quoted from another author as follows: "In all important transactions of life we have to take a leap in the dark....If we decide to leave the riddles unanswered, that is a choice; if we waver in our answer, that too is a choice: but whatever choice we make, we make it at our peril. If a man chooses to turn his back altogether on God and the future, no one can prevent him; no one can show beyond a reasonable doubt that he is mistaken."[7]

By the same line of reasoning, we cannot prove that the Christian is right or wrong either. *THE TRUTH OF FAITH ALWAYS INVOLVES RISK!* I think this is what Jesus meant when, as we read from Luke, our Lord intimated that even in persecution and exclusion and pain and suffering, Christians, regardless of their circumstances could choose to *"LEAP FOR JOY"* (6:23), on the basis of *faith or trust*.

Faith and risk are inextricably intertwined. For example, we can't really demonstrate faith in our spouses as long as they are in our presence. That's not faith. Faith is demonstrated in our absence from one another. I am amazed by how *trust and truth and troth are so interrelated*. Parker J. Palmer has pointed out how the word *truth* comes from the same German root as *troth* or *commitment*, a term traditionally used in marriage vows, "I pledge thee my troth." Marriage is a covenant of mutual accountability, a commitment of mutual fidelity. A spouse commits or pledges troth, which is a special kind of truth and both trust and troth are close to truth. Some more important *TRIVIA* to remember.[8] Faith in a marriage is risking that trust and troth and truth in another person. So is friendship.

Another example could be taken from parent-child relationships. We can't say we have faith in our sons and daughters and then keep them locked up in their rooms. That's not faith or trust. Faith involves risk when they're out of our sight, on a date, using the family car or away at school. *If there isn't any uncertainty or risk, there is no faith!*

The ultimate human moment is the moment of decision, deciding to take that "leap of faith," or to "launch ourselves in moments of despair," even to "leap for joy"—knowing that though to the best of our ability we've done the right thing—to use a country western metaphor—"we might be done wrong," though we did right.

Because of this understanding of *THE TRUTH OF FAITH* as basic trust in God as trustworthy. And because of our *CHRISTIAN* understanding that this trustworthy God is always involved with us in this world—we can risk ourselves in faith, in service, in relationships, in mission. We can *LEAP FORWARD FAITHFULLY*. But first we must take that big step, that leap of faith ourselves that is necessary if we are to find faith, accept the truth and live accordingly.

In the Book of the Acts of the Apostles, parallel Peter and Paul episodes involve the healing of a lame man, who is heard shouting and leaping for joy. Everyone wondered what had happened to him. It wasn't some mysterious healing power associated with Jesus' name, but the lame man's faith in the powerful presence of God, which he discovered when he finally took that leap of faith for himself.

This morning, if there should be a spiritually lame person present, if that one person can be inspired to take that all important leap of faith, we will have used our bonus day this leap year of our Lord A.D. 1992 well having made an important difference worthy of our best efforts.

This much and no more I know for sure this day or any day. God is always faithful and can be trusted. Thanks be unto God.

PART II

– THE FUTURE –
HOPE and WAY

THE WAY OF HOPE

A traveler in Switzerland once asked a boy standing by the roadside, "Where is Kanderstag?" The boy shook his head and replied, "I don't know where Kanderstag is. I've never been there, but I can show you 'the way' that leads there."

That's a lot better than seeing where you would like to go and being told, "Sorry, there's no way, you can't get there from here."

Throughout the ages the persistent plea of humanity has been for God not only to show us mercy and steadfast love (Psalm 17:7; 85:7), but to show us the way, as Moses prayed, "If I have found favor in thy sight, show me now thy ways...."(Exodus 33:13) Such "Show me your way, O Lord!" pleas are epitomized by the ancient Psalmist, who wrote,

> "Teach me thy *way*, O Lord,
> that I may walk in thy *truth*." (Psalm 86:11)
> "Teach me thy *way*. O Lord;
> and lead me on a level path." (Psalm 27:11)

> "O my God, in thee I trust....
> Make me to know thy *ways*, O Lord;
> teach me thy *paths*.
> Lead me in thy *truth*, and teach me,
> for thou art the God of my salvation;
> for thee I wait all the day long." (Psalm 25:2, 4-5)

> "Thou dost show me the path of life; in thy presence
> there is fullness of joy..." (Psalm 16:11)

This sermon was delivered February 21, 1993 at First Federated Church, Peoria, Illinois, following the reading of portions of Romans 5:1-5; 8:18-25, 35, 37-39; 12:12 and 15:13.

The important metaphor of "the way" that leads us—as Christians or "followers of the way"—and the fact that the word *trivia* originally and literally meant "three-ways"—or, better yet, where three ways converged to create a *cross*-roads, have all been introduced previously. The temporal framework we have been using for understanding Christianity started with the PAST in Part I, which focused on "The Truth of Faith."

Faith and Truth are Past realities, in our personal religious experience and our historically rooted Christianity. The fact of the CROSS, the fact of Jesus Christ, the fact of the presence of God in our lives, constitute spiritual *truth* for us and the very basis and beginning of our *faith*. This is one way of understanding Christianity, which the dogma of the Trinity illustrates for us.

...Then I told probably the funniest joke I've ever heard about the Trinity. For those of you who weren't here, you'll have to ask someone who was here to tell it to you sometime....

Well, actually, I didn't tell any joke about the Trinity. I don't know any. I don't think there are any. I just wanted to make you feel you missed something if you weren't here...And you did, but it wasn't a Trinity joke.

* * * * *

This morning in Part II, I want us to focus on the FUTURE, and two key concepts pertaining to the FUTURE, namely, the *way* from John 14 and *hope* from I Corinthians 13.

FAITH AND TRUTH put us on the Christian path or the WAY. and the way is always ahead of us, going before us, out in front of us. The sign of our being put on the path is our baptism, which is our acknowledgement of *FAITH AND TRUTH*. From that point on we're on our Christian way, our spiritual journey, and the metaphor of a pilgrim, a traveller, a way-farer, a *viator*, is a major way of understanding our Christian *life*. Our *faith* is ever transformed into *hope* as we progress along the path of *life*. That transformation is accomplished by means of another concept, *love*, which is our topic for a future sermon. *So tune into TRI-VIA PART III. next Sunday, same time, same place.*

Paul explained this transformation with profound foresight. He suggested that once—B.C.—namely Before we became Christians, we "had no hope" which meant we were—as he said—"without God in the world." (Ephesians 2:12), but now since we have received Christ, our *faith* is the basis for our *hope*. There is that remarkable phrase found in Colossians that speaks of "this mystery, which is Christ in you, the *hope* of glory."(1:27). Again, profound Pauline insight and foresight.

We pass over these phrases as so many words, if we bother with the Biblical witness at all, but "this mystery, which is Christ in us," describes our *faith*, which is our single source of *hope*. We live in the present—in the middle—in between the times—looking backward in *faith* and forward in *hope*.

Now our *hope* is primarily proximate, immediate, though it also has an ultimate component. It is proximate, because the one thing we all need in order to survive from moment to moment and from day to day is hope. Wrote Pope on Hope, not the pontiff, but the poet:

> "Hope springs eternal in the human breast: Man never is, but always to be blest."[1]

The indomitable will to survive, the human struggle to continue, to persevere against overwhelming odds, that drive is amazingly powerful. But it is more than animal instinct. Because in humans *to destroy either one's faith or one's hope can destroy a person's life*, because there would be nothing to live for, look forward to. No tomorrow, no future.

Proximate hope is all important. Hope for a job, hope for health, hope for recovery, hope for a spouse, a family member, a friend, hope for justice and peace, hope for Bosnia, Serbia, Croatia, Cambodia, Slovenia, Liberia, Macedonia, Somalia,

Armenia, Peoria—(There must be something unusual that connects all these places that end in *ia*?)—hope for human improvement, fair treatment, balanced judgement, hope for harmonious relationships between races and classes and genders and ethnic groups and generations.

HOPE LEADS US ON THE WAY!
HOPE KEEPS US GOING!
HOPE HELPS US TO KEEP MOVING FORWARD, SEEKING A BETTER TOMORROW!

Of course, there is such a thing as false hope, which for our secular friends is hope not based on reality. For Christians false hope is hope not based on realistic faith. As such, hope is not only wistful longing, wishful thinking, or empty-ethereal dreaming, it can be harmful and destructive, unless it is built on a solid foundation and grounded in spiritual reality. From Paul's perspective only the Christian can be an optimist regarding this world and this life, for Christians alone have the means of coping with whatever happens, knowing that whatever happens is not the ultimate end.

For the Christian there is always ultimate hope, a final hope that takes us beyond the limitations of our earthly way, beyond the confines of history. Every life involves times when hope is not abandoned, but must be adjusted to a life-long process of experiencing various losses, the final loss being this life itself. The end of this life involves making a transfer from our proximate hopes to our ultimate hope that in some mysterious way, consciousness will continue in a new form, that our spirits, our selves, our souls, are all intertwined eternally with God. Only the Christian can regard death with some semblance of serenity and earthly tragedy with some semblance of equanimity— *both because our hope is based on faith.* We know from whence we came—that's again the *"The Truth of Faith"* and, consequently, we know where we're going—that's *"The Way of Hope."*

* * * * *

A quick review of our New Testament illustrates how future-filled it is with ultimately hopeful ideas:

(l) There is *hope of the resurrection of the dead*,[2] That's not the way we have become accustomed to thinking about hope, is it? We are more immortality minded. But resurrection is the New Testament way. We can look forward to the resurrection because Christ is already resurrected and our life is sealed with His in Spirit and Sacrament.

(2) Secondly, there is *hope of the glory of God* (Romans 5:2). To share that glory is in our future; that is what belief in Jesus Christ involves. Because, again, our lives and His are intertwined. "Now we see in a mirror dimly, but then face to face."(I Corinthians 13:12)

(3) Moreover, there is also *hope of righteousness* (Galatians 5:5), which we hardly ever hear anything about. *Righteousness* is Bible talk for right-relationships. Our relationship with God is already guaranteed by the love of God we have already received, which was sealed in the Christ-Event. So there is a basis for our confidence and certainty—not arrogance or audacity—but a peace that passes all understanding that comes with the knowledge that our lives are wrapped up with the *life and love of God*. We are the recipients of the grace of God which we *accept on faith as truth*. That constitutes our hope and gives us courage and strength to face the present and continue on our *way* toward the Future.

(4) Or, we could talk about the *hope of eternal life* (Titus 1:2; 3:7). Not as if life as we know it is something that will last materially forever. We're not talking about something comparable to the half-life of a plutonium atom or the shelf-life of a "Twinkie," but the quality of our life in relation to God. Eternal life is the spiritual life of God shared with us in which to a certain extent we already participate. Our hope of eternal life is a continuation of that spiritual sharing with God we cherish in this life.[3]

All of this somewhat alien and uncomfortable Christian-talk is talk in terms of our future ultimate *hope* that represents a heavenly home at the end of our earthly *way*, based on *faith* and lived in *love*.

* * * * *

By way of illustration, I think the most hope-filled of Christian ideas is the doctrine of *predestination*—reinterpreted.[4] What follows is the result of some theological reflection and plenty of personal and spiritual wrestling. You may or may not agree with me. It may seem like I'm throwing in a real royal ringer here, because the way the doctrine is usually taught and understood is certainly not what I have in mind. At its worst predestination represents the idea that from before the beginning, God determined what was going to happen to creation, history and everything and everyone in it. Some would be saved, others condemned; some would be successful, others would fail. Everything and everyone was tagged and numbered, etc. The doctrine was inextricably tied to Presbyterian thinking and eventually became a Presbyterian scandal. Presbyterians in their radical defense of the sovereignty of God—as if God ever needed their help—proclaimed an all powerful, all knowing, always in control and ultimately unquestionable God. In so doing predestination proponents frequently stepped over the line of reasonable good judgement and ended up affirming that everything that happened in the history of humanity had to happen the way it happened because God willed it to happen that way. What had been written indelibly in eternity must come to pass historically. Nothing anyone could do could change that. Whatever happened was understood to be the unfolding plan of God in time or history. (Which is exactly what most Muslims believe and a fair number of Christians as well.)

Obviously, human freedom and initiative and responsibility are denied in this view, if the who and the what and the where and the why-for of everything has already been determined, which is to say, predestined, or foreordained or predetermined or whatever.

Nevertheless, despite my aversion and alternative understanding, predestination as traditionally presented remains an awfully easy answer and fairly popular explanation for everything that happens by people who believe they are being very faithful. Predestination remains a popular pastime particularly around mortuaries and emergency rooms and now increasingly in living rooms while watching the evening news. How many times have you heard, "His time was up." Or, "It was God's will!" As if God deviously planned this disaster or that disease. There sometimes follows that really big question, "*WHY?*" Or, "How could God allow this or that to happen?" Which is the cue for someone to pull out the predestination skeleton from the Presbyterian closet and dust it off for discussion purposes, offering it as the answer for anything and everything unfortunate and catastrophic.

"When your time comes, you gotta go," doesn't explain anything. All that is said is that whatever happened had to happen because it happened. And to involve God as the cause and to think that represents great faith, I think, is inexcusable ignorance and only makes matters worse. As if God finally decides (or decided long ago) the time and place and means of our departure, the when, where and how of every disaster and any additional special burdens for us to bear. The flip side of all this —are comments such as "God doesn't give us more than we can bear." Such explanations convey little *HOPE OR FAITH*. At best they represent the pessimistic resignation of condemned prisoners standing before their executioner waiting for the ax to fall. These tragically unfortunate, but popular, presentations of predestination make God the most capricious of calculating tyrants, with a long list of names checked off one by one. God's decisions sometimes eliminate whole groups by means of cosmic "cleansing" whereas floods and earthquakes are only referred to as "acts of God," a phrase I find particularly offensive and infuriating, but frequently used by the press and insurance people when they have no answers either.

* * * * *

Our God is not conjuring up greater and greater catastrophes, despite the developments of modern history with its increasingly more efficient technological means of destruction. This popular kind of sloppy theological thinking rationalizes and legitimizes historical and personal catastrophes as if they are all part of God's will and work. No wonder religion is so suspect and counterproductive.

This is not the God we know as Christians nor is this what I mean by PREDESTINATION.

PREDESTINATION is a doctrine of *HOPE* based on *FAITH*.

PREDESTINATION has nothing to do with cosmic score-keeping or checking people in and out of the *LIFE* game.

PREDESTINATION begins and ends with the *LOVE* of God in Jesus Christ—that all those who believe in him and live according to his *WAY* are *PREDESTINED* to be ever in God's care and keeping. (John 14)

PREDESTINATION has nothing to do with how or when or where we'll die.

PREDESTINATION does mean that whenever, wherever, or howsoever we do die and no matter how ignominious or violent our end, no matter what our earthly circumstance may be, *GOD'S LOVE WILL ALWAYS BE WITH US IN CHRIST.*

> Nothing can separate us from the love of God which was and is and ever will be in Jesus Christ our Lord. (Romans 8:39)

PREDESTINATION is a doctrine that best expresses our ultimate hope and our proximate hopes as we travel life's way, because

PREDESTINATION assures us of God's continued presence with us no matter what might happen to us in history or happen to history itself.

PREDESTINATION in no way explains historical events or human experience, it only assures us that regardless of whatever might befall us while on our way or whatever we might bring upon ourselves, including nuclear or ecological annihilation, there is simply no earthly or historical circumstance powerful enough to separate us from *THE LIFE AND LOVE OF GOD IN JESUS CHRIST* in whom we are *PREDESTINED.* Such is *"THE WAY OF HOPE"* based on *"THE TRUTH OF FAITH"* that gives us confidence to face the future knowing God will be there for us even as God has been with us and is with us right now.

Read with me, if you will, a stunning presentation of "The Way of Hope" taken from the eighth chapter of Romans. Wrote the Apostle Paul,

> "Who shall separate us from the love of Christ? Shall tribulation, or distress, or persecution, or famine, or nakedness, or peril, or sword?...No, in all these things we are more than conquerors through him who loved us. For I am sure that neither death, nor life, nor angels, nor principalities, nor things present, nor things to come, nor powers, nor height, nor depth, nor anything else in all creation, will be able to separate us from the love of God in Christ Jesus our Lord." (Romans 35, 37-39)

"Look up and not down;
Look forward and not back;
Look out and not in;
And lend a hand."

Edward Everett Hale
(1822-1909)

"LOOKING BACKWARD" HOPEFULLY!

SCRIPTURE:

"We give thanks to God always for you all, constantly mentioning you in our prayers, remembering before our God and Father your work of faith and labor of love and steadfastness of hope in our Lord Jesus Christ." (I Thessalonians 1:2-3)

"Blessed be the God and Father of our Lord Jesus Christ! By his great mercy we have been born anew to a living hope through the resurrection of Jesus Christ from the dead... Therefore, gird up your minds, be sober, set your hope fully upon the grace that is coming to you at the revelation of Jesus Christ. As obedient children, do not be conformed to the passions of your former ignorance, but as he who called you is holy, be holy yourselves in all your conduct; since it is written, 'You shall be holy, for I am holy...' Through him you have confidence in God, who raised him from the dead and gave him glory, so that your faith and hope are in God." (I Peter 1:3, 13-16, 21)

* * * * *

Indeed our *"faith and our hope are in God"* which is manifested right now in how we live, in our acts of love and kindness, in lending a hand to help build a better world. Whatever idea of the future we may have has to be implemented in the pre-

---

This sermon was delivered June 6, 1993 at First Federated Church, Peoria, Illinois.

sent. Whatever we think about the past—whenever we look back—we do so with an eye always toward tomorrow. We look back in faith, which enables us to look forward in hope and we work toward the fulfillment of that hope in whatever ways we can...given whatever days and years remain for us.[1]

* * * * *

When we administered the Sacrament of Baptism moments ago, you heard me recite William Stidger's little poem. I know most of you automatically thought of tomorrow—

> In the breast of a bulb
> Is the promise of Spring;
> In the little blue egg
> Is a bird that will sing;
> In the soul of the seed
> Is the hope of the sod;
> In the heart of a child
> Is the Kingdom of God.[2]

The idea of a Kingdom of God and our children's future are inextricably intertwined with hope. We long for a time of fairness and kindness and happiness, justice and peace, where cooperation and good will replace conflict and hostility, where equal opportunity is based on ability, where rights are correlated with responsibilities. Where evidence of care and compassion is found and gentleness abounds. How's that for sounding UTOPIAN?

I remind you that Plato's *Republic* was a utopian piece as were various visions of the heavenly city or Heaven itself as described vividly in the Bible. There is, of course, a difference. A lot of historical heavenly talk has been escapist. The idea of another better life in another better place removes from us the necessity of creating a better life here on earth. Nevertheless, both otherworldly visions and thisworldly utopias arose from conditions of discontent when times were terrible.

The word *Utopia* comes from Sir or Saint—whichever you prefer—Thomas More's (1477-1535) famous book of 1516 by that name. The word is straight Greek meaning *no place ou/topos* or "land of nowhere."[3] But it has been suggested that this English philosopher perhaps punned with the prefix *e-u* instead of *o-u*. hence the word may have been intended to describe not only no place but also a *good* place.[4] Utopias are *good places* as More envisioned an imaginary island that had a perfect social and political system. It was a grand dream and scheme, imaginary and impossibly ideal, but deeply desired as an alternative to present reality as he saw it and so conceived as his attempt to right its wrongs.

Another Englishman, later in the 19th century, Samuel Butler (1835-1902) wrote a more satirical utopia entitled *Erewhon* (1872) and later *Erewhon Revisited* (1901), *Erewhon* is "no where" spelled backward. In it he foreshadowed the collapse of Victorian illusions of eternal progress and the demise of the British Empire.[5] He introduced over a hundred years ago a new imaginary religion, he called "Sunchildism." Doesn't that sound like a trendy, contemporary sunbelt cult? This new church had three theological professors named Dr. Hanky and Dr. Panky and Dr. Downie, "all three experts in complicating the simple and in juggling theological hocus-pocus."[6] It's always fun to see how accurate many of the utopian projections really are. Butler in particular seems to have been right on target.

But the utopian novel from which I have taken the sermon idea and title for today is from an American author, Edward Bellamy (1850-1898), who wrote the best-selling book of 1888. Now there is some memorable trivia you will want to store away. In the book Julian West, a young, wealthy Bostonian, after calling on his fiancee, Edith Bartlett, earlier in the evening, found he could not fall asleep. So a physician friend hypnotized him...

West awakened 113 years later in a very very different world. If you think Rip van Winkle was astonished, you can imagine how Julian West must have rubbed his eyes. In contrast to Rip, Julian had preserved his youthful appearance. Soon he fell in love with the great granddaughter of his first fiancee, another Edith no less. On a tour to reacquaint Julian with the city, she explained the cooperative commonwealth that had come into existence while he slept all those years. A marvelous transformation had occurred. Everybody worked and shared alike. It should come as no surprise that most utopias are socialist, with the State understood as the Great Trust. With economic stability and a healthy environment, crime is down, culture is up, all the old evils characterized by ruthless greed are gone.

What started out as "a literary fantasy," for Bellamy, "a fairy tale of social felicity," as he said, soon became a vehicle for changing the world as he tried to create an image of the world the way he wanted it to be.[7] The truth of the matter is, though Bellamy's work radically influenced many changes in the social gospel movement and idealistic reforms in the progressive movement prior to World War I, this century has hardly produced a more humane world. That is our real 20th Century tragedy, but still our present opportunity and hope for the future.

Technologically, we can point to considerable progress, but in the *arena of relationship*, which is what religion addresses, there is a lot of room for much needed improvement. Though I haven't been altogether asleep myself for the past thirty years since first reading Bellamy's book, I can truthfully say, the world in which we are now living has not met even the most minimal of my own personal expectations. Matters and issues I thought would be taken for granted by now have not been addressed and certainly remain unresolved. How innocent or naive or stupid I must have been. Some things just seemed so logical, even self-evident or matters of common sense, like supporting universal education, enforcing zero population growth, becoming more ecologically sensitive and responsible, promoting healthy racial and ethnic understanding, advocating the elimination of drugs, hand-guns, child abuse, etc. And stupidest of all, I believed in a world where greed would be replaced by the common good (which is—by the way—the underlying problem of what should be called these days "greedlock."

* * * * *

This morning I want to read from Bellamy's book because of his absolutely haunting coach metaphor used in the opening pages. It is a stunningly troublesome analysis, but one that warrants our attention. It is as pertinent a parable for 1993 as it was over a hundred years ago when it was written. Here then is how the book begins: *Looking Backward* from 2000 to 1887:

> "Living as we do in the closing year of the twentieth century, enjoying the blessings of a social order at once so simple and logical that it seems but the triumph of common sense, it is no doubt difficult for those whose studies have not been largely historical to realize that the present organization of society is, in its completeness, less than a century old. No historical fact is, however, better established than that till nearly the end of the nineteenth century it was the general belief that the ancient industrial system, with all its shocking social consequences, was destined to last, with possibly a little patching, to the end of time. How strange and well nigh incredible does it seem that so prodigious a moral and material transformation as has taken place since then could have been accomplished in so brief an interval!

> "(Let us) compare society as it then was (in 1873) to a prodigious coach (like a stagecoach) which the masses of humanity were harnessed to (like a team of horses) and dragged toilsomely along a very hilly and sandy road. The driver (of the coach) was hunger, and permitted no lagging, though the pace was necessarily very slow. Despite the difficulty of drawing the coach at all along so hard a road, the top was covered with passengers who never got down, even at the steepest ascents. Those seats on the top were very breezy and comfortable. Well up out of the dust and their occupants could enjoy the scenery at their leisure, or critically discuss the merits of the straining team. Naturally such places were in great demand and the competition for them was keen, everyone seeking as the first end in life to secure a seat on the coach for himself and to leave it to his child

after him. By the rule of the coach a man could leave his seat to whom he wished, but on the other hand, there were many accidents by which (the seat) might at any time be wholly lost. ...the seats were very insecure, and at every sudden jolt of the coach persons were slipping out of them and falling to the ground, where they were instantly compelled to take hold of the rope and help to drag the coach (on which they had before ridden so pleasantly). It was naturally regarded as a terrible misfortune to lose one's seat, and the apprehension that this might happen to them or their friends was a constant cloud upon the happiness of those who rode.

(l) But did they think only of themselves? you ask.

(2) Was not their very luxury rendered intolerable to them by comparison with the lot of their brothers and sisters in the harness, and the knowledge that their own weight added to their toil?

(3) Had they no compassion for fellow beings from whom fortune only distinguished them? Oh, yes; commiseration was frequently expressed by those who rode for those who had to pull the coach, especially when the vehicle came to a bad place in the road, as it was constantly doing, or to a particularly steep hill. At such times, the desperate straining of the team, their agonized leaping and plunging under the pitiless lashing of hunger, the many who fainted at the rope and were trampled in the mire, made a very distressing spectacle, which often called forth highly creditable displays of feeling on the top of the coach. At such times the passengers would call down encouragingly to the toilers of the rope, exhorting them to patience, and holding out hopes of possible compensation in another world for the hardness of their lot, while others contributed to buy salves and liniments for the crippled and injured. It was agreed that it was a great pity that the coach should be so hard to pull and there was a sense of general relief when an especially bad piece of road was gotten over. This relief was not, indeed, wholly on account of the team, for there was always some danger at these bad places of a general overturn in which all would lose their seats.

It must in truth be admitted that the main effect of the spectacle of the misery of the toilers at the rope was to enhance the passengers' sense of the value of their seats upon the coach, and to cause them to hold on to them more desperately than before. If the passengers could only have felt assured that neither they nor their friends would ever fall from the top, it is probable that, beyond contributing to the funds for liniments and bandages, they would have troubled themselves extremely little about those who dragged the coach.

I am well aware that this will appear to the men and women of the twentieth century an incredible inhumanity, but there are two facts, both very curious, which partly explain it. In the first place, it was firmly and sincerely believed that there was no other way in which society could get along, except that the many pulled at the rope and the few rode, and not only this, but that no very radical improvement even was possible, either in the harness, the coach, the roadway, or the distribution of the toil. It had always been as it was, and it always would be so. It was a pity, but it could not be helped, and philosophy forbade wasting compassion on what was beyond remedy.

The other fact is yet more curious, consisting in a singular hallucination which those on the top of the coach generally shared, that they were not exactly like their brothers and sisters who pulled at the rope, *but of finer clay*, in some way belonging to a higher order of beings who might justly expect to be drawn. This seems unaccountable, but, as I once rode on this very coach and shared that very hallucination, I ought to be believed. The strangest thing about the hallucination, was that those who had but just climbed up from the ground, before they had outgrown the marks of the rope upon their hands, began to fall under its influence. As for those whose parents and grandparents before them had been so fortunate as to keep their seats on the top, the conviction they cherished of the essential difference between their sort of humanity and the common people was absolute. The effect of such a delusion in moderating fellow feeling for the suffering of the mass of men...

is obvious. (However, this) indifference...marked my own attitude toward the misery of my brothers."

* * * * *

This amazing document is, of course, a damning indictment of all of us. Oh, we could quickly point to others on top who have far more than we have. Or, we could complain about the irresponsibility of the have-not masses who comprise most of humanity below. Nevertheless, we're the 'haves' who represent the top 2% or 3% of the world's wealth. The fact of the matter is we represent the privileged class—not the poverty stricken. We represent the power elite—not the oppressed. Harassed maybe, but not oppressed. We are the ones sitting on top of Bellamy's coach and complaining about the inadequacy and inefficiency of the system. Periodically, we toss out our tokens and tidbits of care and concern and call it Christian love or mission, but when asked in the name of Christ to consider changing the conditions such as Bellamy described, we all of a sudden become defensive in our outlook, blaming the victim, perhaps even quoting the very words of Jesus,

"For you will always have the poor with you..."
(Mark 14:7)

as if that's the way God intended the world to be. Or worse, that both the toilers of the rope and the sitters on the coach earned and deserved their respective positions.

However we wish to understand ourselves or our situation, we're still a coach rider—top sider. Regardless of race or religion or gender or ethnic origin, we look and act more like brothers and sisters of our fellow top siders than we do with any of those who make up the straining team of humanity whipped by hunger and necessity. As top siders united together, we share our cakes and kippersnacks with grey poupon, while debating the problem below and—sad but true—as long as we can keep talking and keep the coach moving, we can keep from involving ourselves too seriously in the life and death issues of most of the men, women and children of the world that make up the team. Unfortunately, nothing is simple. That we know. And nothing is really new either. These circumstances are as old as human society.

But our Christian *HOPE* promises a new society. That thought suggests an awesome responsibility. Better yet, it is a God given opportunity for us in our time to seek new paradigms regarding the purpose of the church and the Kingdom of God. Occasionally, some top siders are awakened by what might be, or even could be. We glimpse a revelatory vision that is not self-centered or self-serving, but centered on serving others and concerned about doing what might be best for society in general—'the greatest good of the greatest number.'[8] That vision could even be of the Kingdom of God. It's a frightening prospect for us. What will it cost us to think of the greater good? Will it involve relinquishing our coach seats? And just when we could use some spiritual help and reaffirmation, Jesus throws us one of those "lead" life preservers,

> "Whoever seeks to gain his life will lose it, but whoever loses his life will preserve it." (Luke 17:33)

My purpose is not to make us all guilty or miserable or even angry. My purpose is to remind us that

> "to whom much has been given, much will be required." (Luke 13:48)[9]

My purpose is to remind us that

> "where there is no vision, the people perish."(Proverbs 29:18 KJV)

PEOPLE ARE PERISHING!

Christians must be a people of vision, a responsible people with a new paradigm, a people of *HOPE*. I truly believe our Christian obligation is to suggest and to seek those conditions that transcend the self-interest or profit of any particular group. Our God-given goal is to suggest and to seek the greater good, the common good.

One way to rethink the Kingdom of God and the greater/common good is to do for all children, what we want for and do for our own children. For would not God want what is good for all children? If we project our hopes for our own children into the future, would that vision not represent a new paradigm for understanding the Kingdom of God? Now the ringer is that the church is the vehicle through which primarily the purposes of God are realized. The church is committed to such visionary concepts and idealistic causes as the Kingdom of God and the good of all children. Working toward that end is a pretty big order for an institution whose health and influence is in considerable jeopardy already. The church is hard-pressed even to find unanimity in accepting one another inside, not to mention accepting those outside. And we are aware of many other ecclesiastical difficulties.

Yet here we are this morning, sensing the presence of God together, genuinely seeking God's purposes for us, looking backward and looking forward in relation to our children and grandchildren and the human family in general. Have not each of us at one time or another—especially in rearing our families and identifying ourselves with the Christian family—thought of building a better world? Christ literally knocked at our door, and at one point each of us opened the door and received Him. We have all acknowledged at some time or another that *Christ is the hope of the world*,

> "the hope of all the ends of the earth, and of the farthest seas," (Psalm 65:5)

and that we are harbingers of that *HOPE* as Christians and churches that use the name of Christ. *We literally exist to help make hope happen!*

Our Christian task is truly utopian, to transform *no place* into some *good place for all the children*. Ours is the responsibility to create the Kingdom of God to the best of our fallible ability. Or, if we prefer a new paradigm, in place of the Kingdom of God, an environment conducive to the well-being of all the world's children.

Ours is indeed a big task. Unfortunately, most of the people in the world including those like us who understand ourselves to be religious probably would well respond like a skeptical Glaucon did to Socrates in Plato's great utopia. Socrates had been describing eloquently the ideal way of life in the ideal society, when Glaucon suddenly interrupted.

"Socrates, I do not believe that there is such a (Kingdom) of God as you describe anywhere on earth."

To which Socrates responded,

"Whether such a kingdom exists in heaven or ever will exist on earth, the wise man will live after the manner of that kingdom, having nothing to do with any other, and in so looking upon it, will set his own house in order."[10]

May God help us to set ourselves and our own houses and churches in order. Help us to hold fast to a vision for the future that includes all the children. Help us to be faithful as we look backward and hopeful as we look forward. And in all our present living—be LOVING!

> "For our faith and our hope (remain ever) in God." (I Peter 1:21)

Thanks be unto God.   Amen.

Hope of the world, thou Christ of great compassion,
Speak to our fearful hearts by conflict rent.
Save us, thy people, from consuming passion,
Who by our own false hopes and aims are spent.

Hope of the world, God's gift from hightest heaven,
Bringing to hungry souls the bread of life,
Still let thy Spirit unto us be given
To heal earth's wounds and end her bitter strife.

Hope of the world, afoot on dusty highways,
Showing to wandering souls the path of light,
Walk thou beside us lest the tempting byways
Lure us away from thee to endless night.

Hope of the world, who by thy cross didst save us
From death and dark despair, from sin and guilt,
We render back the love thy mercy gave us;
Take thou our lives and use them as thou wilt.

Georgia Harkness
(1891-1974)

A new friend of the author during her Claremont
retirement years. She was an author, teacher,
United Methodist minister and prominent church
leader whose influence continues through her
books and poems.

THE HOPE OF THE WORLD

PART I. INTRODUCTION

At the 132nd Commencement Exercise of Washington University on May 14, 1993, the undergraduate senior class president, Brian Buckles, a young man from a small Illinois town, gave an address in which he thanked the university for imparting *knowledge* to the student body. But then he proceeded to chastise the faculty and chide the administration. He took them to task for not teaching morality nor inculcating spiritual values without which there can be no true knowledge or *wisdom*. *Wisdom*, he went on, involves spiritual values and belief in God, a reality that had not been a part of his formal university education as if unknown to the faculty, absent from the curriculum and unwelcome on campus. He was given a standing ovation by many in the crowd.[1] We didn't attend that ceremony, but when we arrived, even casual conversation the rest of that day involved what it meant to be *WISE*.

To our amazement the principle speaker at the medical school graduation ceremony held later that afternoon at a downtown St. Louis hotel, also talked about values, spiritual values, even God again. He talked about modeling and his mother. I particularly remember how he said we value a Reebok more than we do reading a book, how things are all twisted in our minds to the extent that sports and entertainment figures are more esteemed than those who utilize their brains in expanding scientific knowledge and serving humanity. His topic was "The

---

Portions of this sermon were delivered at First Federated Church, Peoria, Illinois on February 3, 1991 and on June 6, 1993, entitled "Wisdom is Justified by All Her Children!" (Luke 7:35)

Doctor's Mission." I was impressed! Dr. Benjamin S. Carson, Sr., Director of the Division of Pediatric Neurosurgery at Johns Hopkins University is a *wise* man and he shared with us *wisdom*.[2]

Subsequently, I found myself thinking again about a favorite theme, *wisdom*, a word which for me has come to mean "the presence of God combined with a concern for children." What do you think, when you hear the words, *wise and wisdom*?

Certainly, if as the Psalmist suggests,

> "The fool says in his heart, 'There is no God,'" (14:1 or 53:1, 10:4)

then it must be the wise man who knows God in his heart. (cf. Proverbs 28:26) The Book of Proverbs abounds in encouraging *wisdom*.

> "The beginning of wisdom is this: Get *wisdom*, and whatever you get, get insight." (4:7)

More familiar is the Proverb that tells us,

> "The fear of the Lord is the beginning of wisdom, and the knowledge of the Holy One is insight." (9:10)

I should add that "fear" should be understood in terms of a "healthy respect." (cf. 15:33)

I found myself again returning to a favorite passage from Luke which allows us to correlate the *wisdom* that acknowledges the presence of God with the *wisdom* that demonstrates our concern for children—those who represent *OUR HOPE FOR TOMORROW*, better yet, *THE HOPE OF THE WORLD*.

My text comes from that enigmatic line found in the seventh chapter of Luke where the power of God's presence in Jesus of Nazareth is being offered as proof to the disciples of John the Baptist that Jesus was definitely the one sent from God, the one for whom they were preparing *the way*. The chapter is pivotal, dealing with the relationship between these two contending prophets, John and Jesus, the whole point being that John's disciples did not need to look any further for confirmation. Jesus was the One.[3]

The chapter opens with the story of the Roman centurion's slave sick and near death—who miraculously receives the *gift of health*.

Then in the verses that immediately follow, another manifestation of God's powerful presence in Jesus of Nazareth is described, a widow's only son, who had died, miraculously receives the *gift of life*.

Hear now a portion of this morning's Scripture lesson beginning with verse 16 and continuing through verse 28:

THE READER IS ASKED TO READ
LUKE 7:16-28

EXPOSITION:

In an age that looked for the prophet, who would finally initiate a new order—referred to as the Kingdom of God or the Kingdom of Heaven—

In an age when these two men were in a kind of prophetic competition, Jesus said that John the Baptist represented the pinnacle of the old order—

Nobody ever born was any better; however, in the new order, John was less than the very least.

If John were the greatest of the old order and there was no central place for him in the kingdom, whose would the kingdom be? To whom belonged the new order that both men proclaimed, but that Jesus initiated?

No one was prepared for Jesus' answer and neither are we today. *The new order belonged to children!* This was an unanticipated surprise. What a jolt, like an earthquake, whose aftershocks are still occurring, a thunderbolt whose reverberations are still rumbling around. The historical period in which both John and Jesus lived was hardly known for its rigorous defense of the rights of children, for its response to their needs or for its benevolent treatment. Think of Herod's slaughter of innocent children, shortly after the birth of Jesus (Matthew 2:16-18).

Children weren't recognized as persons; they were property, considered chattel like cattle. In an age when even his own disciples rebuked him for bothering with children, Jesus said,

> "Let the children come to me and do not hinder them; for to such *belongs* the Kingdom of God." (Luke 18:16)

The new order belonged to the children! Acknowledgement of that fact can be seen as rudimentary WISDOM.

What a most unusual and revolutionary social idea, a radical reversal in thought and conduct that remains enigmatic to this very day. In diametric opposition to his contemporaries, peers and the spirit of his historical period, Jesus "lifted up"[4] children and placed them in the center of his teaching about the Kingdom of God.

Moreover, recall how he told his listeners that

> "whoever does not receive the Kingdom of God like a child shall not enter it." (18:17)

> "whoever humbles himself like (a) child...is the greatest in the kingdom of heaven." (Matthew 18:4)

> "whoever receives a child (because of Jesus' commendation of children) receives Jesus." (v. 5.)

On the other hand, "whoever causes" a child to suffer or stumble or sin,

> "it would be better for him to have a great millstone fastened round his neck and to be drowned in the depth of the sea." (v. 6.)

Rather drastic punishment for those who neglect, abandon, abuse and batter children. What did Jesus mean? What are the implications for us and for the church that bears His Name? What does this parable of the children in the market place say to us about our important parental role and supportive congregational and educational responsibilities? I don't claim to know specifically what Jesus meant. I don't have a sack full of ready-made answers to be dispensed here and there as needed.

However, there is no question in my mind that children were of central importance in Jesus' life and teaching. That's clear enough. And, certainly, there can be no question that there are important implications for our understanding of the nature and mission of the church today that issue from His teaching about children and the kingdom that demand our attention and best efforts. Because Children and the Kingdom of God can be correlated with what Jesus—"the way, the truth and the life"—said about "faith and hope and love." To make that correlation real is our Christian responsibility and opportunity to change the world while being *WISE* and imparting *WISDOM*.

* * * * *

Hear now the rest of this morning's Gospel lesson!
LUKE 7:31-35

SCRIPTURE:

"to what then shall I compare the men of this generation, and what are they like? They are like children sitting in the marketplace and calling to one another.

'We piped to you, and you did not dance; we wailed, and you did not weep.'

For John the Baptist has come eating no bread and drinking no wine; and you say, 'He has a demon.' The Son of man has come eating and drinking; and you say, 'Behold, a glutton and a drunkard, a friend of tax collectors and sinners!' Yet wisdom is justified by all her children."

PART II.   INTRODUCTION

In this seventh chapter, Luke continued his discussion of the prophetic relationship between John and Jesus, between the old order and the new. Luke compared the people's response to children, playing little marketplace games, which we might call, "weddings and funerals," perhaps like we used to play "cops and robbers" or "cowboys and indians." It's not altogether clear what the game was all about, or what Jesus meant by the illustration. But it appears that either the children couldn't agree on the game to be played, or it was a matter of their not knowing how to play according to the rules or other's expectations. Perhaps it was more a matter of their refusal to cooperate. One group saying, "Come on, let's play weddings," But some potential players didn't feel like being happy. So someone else suggested, "Then let's play funerals." But no one wanted to feel sad either.

At any rate, Jesus' generation was being compared with a confusing children's game, which illustrated the indecision and irrationality of those people who either couldn't or wouldn't make up their minds about John or Jesus. Our generation is certainly comparably confused. We can't make up our mind about values, priorities, commitments, right and wrong, or even God, just as long ago people couldn't make up their minds about Jesus and John.

Jesus chided the people for not recognizing in John the Baptist the power of God and the prophetic purposes of God. "What did you expect of a prophet like John? What were you looking for out their in the wilderness? A prophet? Indeed! None better than he. But you failed to recognize in him the power of God and the prophetic purposes of God." Instead you said, "He has a demon; he's crazy!"

"And what did you expect to find in me? A prophet too and more! But you call me a glutton, a drunkard and other nasty names. You tried to make John into an ascetic and me into a profligate. What kind of a game is this generation playing?

Looking for God and the Kingdom and refusing to recognize the powerful presence of God, when it's right in front of you; God's work in the world right there before your very eyes, but you simply cannot see."

Then, as if in conclusion or, perhaps, frustration, even desperation in being rejected by so many of his contemporaries or maybe even resignation, though not without *HOPE*, Jesus said,

> *"WISDOM IS JUSTIFIED BY ALL HER CHILDREN."*
> (v. 35.)

It's that single line that literally will not let go of me. It has been haunting me for a long time.

> *"WISDOM IS JUSTIFIED BY ALL HER CHILDREN."*
> (v. 35.)

And I hope it will haunt you as well, mothers and fathers and church members. Not immobilize, but prod and probe and inspire. So what does this verse mean? What is the *connection between children and wisdom and the hope of the world*? What's the point of the parable? I'd like to mention four possibilities for us to consider this morning:

EXPOSITION:

I. In the context of the chapter it was the children who believed in Him, who received Him, who accepted Him, who sensed in His presence the power of God. They were the ones who openly took "no offense"...v. 23) at Him. Obviously, for Luke *wisdom* was the enthusiastic acceptance of Jesus and His Kingdom like children. This is probably the primary meaning and interpretation of our challenging text:

> *"WISDOM IS JUSTIFIED BY ALL HER CHILDREN."*

But that's not all it means. I may be moving too rapidly to other secondary meanings, but I do so, believing that children's acceptance of Jesus—spontaneously, exuberantly, totally—constitutes the *wisdom* Luke is writing about.

II. However, beyond that, we can indicate that there is a parallel version of the story found in Matthew. There the same story is told, but the punch line substitutes *"deeds"* for *"children."*

"WISDOM IS JUSTIFIED BY ALL HER *DEEDS*."
(11:19)

Matthew's emphasis was more pragmatic, more result and action oriented. The results or consequences of Jesus' presence and power spoke for themselves. The Gospel reader is asked to consider the poor, the blind, the lame, the deaf, even the dead. *Wisdom* for Matthew amounted to acknowledging *the one who had done these very deeds in their presence* and seeing in Him and in these acts, the power and purposes of God at work in the world. The evidence cited was thought to be sufficient proof. That was Matthew's point.

Much like the deeds referred to in both Matthew and Luke, so the contemporary church that bears Christ's name must translate our Christian claims of care and concern for all people—especially all children—into deeds that make a difference, that touch and change lives. The Church of Christ exists for mission, to fulfill in and through us God's purposes for all people.

It's not what the church ever says nearly as much as what the church does in the name of Christ that really counts. So it is with children. There is no more damming statement nor indictment of parents or any of us than to tell children, "Do as I say, not as I do!" It is what we DO that makes the difference, namely, DEEDS!

III. But the single line still has more to give. There's a clear indication here that *wisdom* involves a correlation between children and deeds. When we put Matthew and Luke's versions together, the sentence could well be asking,

"What is the church doing for children?"

"What should the church be doing for children?"

Is a family support system being suggested subtly? A course going to be offered soon on family values? Day care or even night care offered for working mothers? Is this sermon related to health care for infants or adolescents and mandatory immunization for all children? Family planning, early screening programs and sex education in the public schools? Or, perhaps, we should be limiting and licensing parents. Taxing parents for having children rather than giving them tax credits? Does this involve nutritional needs or Christian nurture?

Now there's one that warrants our attention, Christian nurture! I am reminded of recent public school graduations across the country. How is God related to public school graduation exercises?

I was asked to give an invocation at a graduation this year and then later unasked. But on the night of the actual ceremony—though not officially on the program—I was asked to say a few words in the spot normally occupied by the invocation. As I stood before the group I didn't want to get the school board into trouble, nor offend anyone, because public prayer is a sensitive issue. But I also wanted to thank God and the parents and teachers for their example and the students for their accomplishments. So I said,

"I want to pray, but find I cannot, because of the recent Supreme Court decision."

One woman in the audience interrupted and asked, "If you could pray, what would you say?"

I responded by saying, "If I had been allowed to pray I would have said something like this and I would have invited all of you to join me. Then I proceeded to pray...

That seems so trivial a matter and, perhaps, inconsequential to many, if not foolish. But it is really important and represents the *wisdom* that recognizes the presence of God at work in the world, a reality whose exclusion from public education and ceremonies where children are involved, though a complicated issue, is without excuse.

Given the magnitude of complex children's needs, a complex political environment that is incessantly wrestling with what is correct or incorrect as the case may be, how should the church be involved? We're overwhelmed many times and don't know where to begin, because there is so much that needs to be done. Certainly the church must become more involved in *affirming the wisdom of God and the wisdom of children*. Because in that correlation is *THE HOPE OF THE WORLD*. If the church is not wise in relation to its belief about God and children, there is little hope for the future. But I am confident that the church has and will respond with even greater vigor. There is no more logical starting point in any community than the Christian Church in addressing the needs of children, for we are already committed to the kingdom of God and to the needs of all children. We in the church not only say we care, based on our Christian faith and hope and love, we do care and we demonstrate our care in deeds. This has been confirmed over and over again in my own pastoral experience.[5]

I'm not suggesting that individual churches need to start individual projects for children in a very complicated environment, rather involvement in cooperative efforts is so desperately needed in every community in America. The destruction or deterioration of the family can be easily documented. The church is in a unique position to affirm the family and upbuild the home, when even parents themselves seem hell-bent on their self-destruction. Physical violence and emotional and sexual abuse including incest are not crimes committed by strangers. These are family matters. We should avoid easy rationalization as to the cause or the cure. Nevertheless, as Christians, as parents and as adults, we should ever be aware of the consequences of our actions on all the children.

One of the most startling statistics I know, I read over a decade ago in the *Newsletter* of the American Orthopsychiatric Association,[6] where it was announced that less than one in ten children born back then would be reared to age 18 in the home of both their biological parents. Shortly thereafter I was on a plane and not wanting to visit, but the passenger next to me—from Philadelphia no less—was persistent in his brotherly overtures to talk. After being tolerably polite and telling him what I did, I shared that statistic and suggested he pick at random ten families in his own inner circle of family and friends and test it. He was silent for some time while I was thinking how cleverly I had handled that situation. I had even returned to my book. When suddenly he announced, "You're wrong. It's three in ten."

If the result was three out of ten in his elite circle, we can imagine what it must be for the general public. And, certainly, the last decade has not improved that startling statistic. Children need above all else, good parents as their primary models to imitate. They need to know what a responsible adult is, how responsible husbands and wives relate, how responsible mothers and fathers act, Without good parents everything else we try to do for children is at best piecemeal and patch-work. The starting point for any church in correlating children and deeds and wisdom and hope is best accomplished by getting back to the spiritual fundamentals of Christian marriage and family, good parenting and healthy homes.

IV. Ah, You thought we were finished. But the implications of our tenacious little text this morning are legion. The possible meanings of *"WISDOM IS JUSTIFIED BY ALL HER CHILDREN AND/OR DEEDS"* have not been exhausted. There is yet another thought, a fourth implication. In fact, the really haunting aspect of this single sentence has yet to be mentioned. Our verse contains a prophetic message addressed to us or to any age. For the *wisdom* of any age is only as good as the next generation's interpretation. The hope of any generation rests with its children, so perhaps it was uttered as a proverb, a prophetic oracle bent on future vindication, a future fulfilled by the children to whom the kingdom was already promised. Isn't that our *HOPE* as well, as we rear our own children? Isn't that something to think about—given the deplorable circumstances in which so many children exist today? Just trying to survive can be a great victory for a majority of the world's children?

We parents hope that our children will consider our own parenting wise. If our wisdom is only as efficacious as our children's interpretation, the question that troubled me when I became a father was how wise a parent would I be? And now, *was*? What will my children think of me? We judge the generation that preceded us and we will be judged in turn by those who succeed us. Our best efforts will only be as good as what our children choose to believe about us. Like the proverbial sins of previous fathers (and mothers) falling on present sons and daughters, so it is with contemporary WISDOM, for better or worse, falling on those who follow us.

WISDOM is not justified by the academic or scientific or professional community or any college or university, the political majority, the courts or press or popular opinion polls. WISDOM is not justified by psychologists, psychometrists, social workers or psychiatrists. WISDOM is justified—*ONLY BY HER CHILDREN*—tomorrow, or next-week or next year, but always sometime in the future. So the problem that is indelibly written into this prophetic line and which is so disturbing to our complacency is whether what we call WISDOM today will be considered wise or ignorant, sinful or hopeful by the children of tomorrow.

What kind of a legacy are we leaving them? How wise are we today in our parenting, in our social planning, in our prioritizing, in our adult modeling? Yes, especially our role modeling? How wise are we in our Christian nurturing, our passing Christian faith on to the next generation? That's the message that needs to be heard. Clearly, the hope of any generation rests with the children of the next generation, a future that is not only promised, but already belongs to them. That's what this prophetic line from Jesus must mean.

I close with a favorite saying that our daughters heard with such frequency and intensity at times that they not only committed it to memory, they became extremely tired of hearing it. But it remains good advise for us all.

> The ignorant never learn.
> The smart learn by their own mistakes.
> The wise learn by other's mistakes.
> Therefore, be wise!

If, indeed, *"WISDOM IS JUSTIFIED BY ALL HER CHILDREN"* and *"BY ALL HER DEEDS,"* may God help us all to be wise in all we do for all children. In Jesus name.   Amen.

A PRAYER FOR CHILDREN

We pray for children
 who sneak popsicles before supper,
 who erase holes in math workbooks,
 who can never find their shoes.
And we pray for those
 who stare at photographers form behind barbed wire,
 who can't bound down the street in a new pair of sneakers,
 who never "counted potatoes,"
 who are born in places we wouldn't be caught dead,
 who never go to the circus,
 who live in an X-rated world.
We pray for children
 who bring us sticky kisses and fistfuls of dandelions,
 who hug us in a hurry and forget their lunch money.
We pray for those
 who never get dessert,
 who have no safe blanket to drag behind them,
 who watch their parents watch them die,
 who can't find any bread to steal,]
 who don't have any rooms to clean up,
 whose pictures aren't on anybody's dresser,
 whose monsters are real.
We pray for children
 who spend all their allowance before Tuesday,
 who throw tantrums in the grocery store and pick at their food,
 who like ghost stories,
 who shove dirty clothes under the bed, and never rinse out the tub,
 who get visits from the tooth fairy,
 who don't like to be kissed in front of the carpool,
 who squirm in church or temple and scream in the phone,
 whose tears we sometimes laugh at and whose smiles can make us cry.
And we pray for those
 whose nightmares come in the daytime,
 who will eat anything,
 who have never seen a dentist,
 who aren't spoiled by anybody,
 who go to bed hungry and cry themselves to sleep,
 who live and move, but have no being
We pray for children who want to be carried
 and for those who must,
 for those we never give up on and for those
 who don't get a second chance.
For those we smother...and for those who will grab the hand of anybody kind enough to offer it.[7]

Ina Hughs

87

He is the Way.
Follow Him through the land of unlikeness;
you will see rare beasts and have unique adventures.

He is the Truth.
Seek Him in the Kingdom of anxiety; you will come to a
great city that has expected your return for years.

He is the Life.
Love Him in the world of the flesh and at your marriage
all its occasions shall dance for joy.

W. H. Auden
(1907-1973)

PRISONERS OF HOPE

The challenge to anyone with the audacity to stand up here week after week is to challenge any one who has the patience to sit where you do week after week. But we share so much in common including our commitment to Christ and the Christian Church and the desire to make our faith work in our individual lives and in our life together. So the experience is not without its rewards and benefits, because our shared experience makes a difference.

Ironically, I thought about all this a few months ago while viewing the reunion of a conglomeration of comedians who once comprised "Laugh-In," a reunion which I didn't find all that laughable. Perhaps some of you saw it too? Years ago, back in the late sixties that show was rather risque with lots of exposed body surfaces and not so subtle innuendo, double entendre and suggestive allusions. It was praised by its fans, condemned by its critics and thrived on controversy.

One "very interesting" part of "Laugh-In" that I remember and enjoyed was an award called the "Fickle Finger of Fate" given weekly to some person or group that represented a political perspective not appreciated by the show's writers—something that contradicted what they deemed appropriate. They sought to point out contradictions as they saw them, and above all else expose hypocrisy wherever found—hopefully in high places. A

This sermon was originally entitled "The UNtriumphant beginning of a TRIUMPHANT End" and delivered on Palm Sunday, April 4, 1993, with Old Testament lessons taken from Zechariah 9:9-12, Isaiah 40:1-2; 61:7 and a New Testament reading from Luke 19:28-48.

somewhat strange introduction for a Palm Sunday sermon, but perhaps a way that can help provide some new insights and hopefully new appreciation of an old, familiar theme.

If the award was still given, this week we could give it posthumously to those people long ago, back in Jerusalem, who hailed our Lord, and shouted "Hosannas" and "Hoorays," "Hats off to the King," "the Man of the Hour," "the Messiah,"—the one expected to restore Israel to her rightful place and redeem her people. Hey, those people would be right on target today with rampant nationalism raising its close-minded head all over the globe. Millions of people are just waiting for the right leader. And, "Watch out, any leader with the audacity to emerge!" "Watch out, any self proclaimed savior seeking to mobilize or stabilize the masses and clean up the messes." Perhaps, that's what a Messiah does? Clean up the messes of the masses. "Be careful, Mr or Mrs Messiah!" Whenever you deal with massive messes and especially the emancipation of those masses, be very careful, for fame works faster than Fleet and is terribly ...*FICKLE.*

* * * * *

A second thought about Palm Sunday pertains to our traditional Old Testament reading this morning. I found myself reflecting on that phrase Zechariah used—when he referred to his people as *"prisoners of hope."* What a poignant expression. Of course, the prophet was proclaiming to those prisoners who had long-suffered in exile that their hopes would soon be vindicated and they would be returning triumphantly and reclaiming their class, status and power. The promised land and prominence and their restored proper place: all were imminent. So close you could almost touch it or taste it—that grand and glorious messianic kingdom when God would rule on earth and everything would be made right. And the ground for their hopefulness was that covenant God had once made with their ancestors way back during the Exodus at Sinai, sealed by the sprinkling of blood. (Exodus 24:7-8)

All that ancient symbolism remains our symbolism to this day. It's all here packed into this week—intact—whether for the ancient Israelites or the Israelites in exile, or the crowds lining the streets of Jerusalem that first Palm Sunday or in how many places around the globe today? It's in the wind; we can feel it. Moreover, in most cases, it is understood that God has promised the age that is about to dawn. Right?

Now you may wonder as I do, how anyone or group can be so absolutely certain that their hopes are truly valid? For that matter how can we be sure our hopes will

> "not disappoint us?" (Romans 5:5)

The only assurance we ever have is what Paul suggested in that passage from Romans,

> "...because God's love has been poured into our hearts through the Holy Spirit which has been given to us."

I believe that and base my own hopes upon such faith. Probably the Branch Davidians and Gay and Lesbian Christians, and Pro-Life and Pro-Choice activists and Episcopalians and Serbians do too. The point is this! Are we not all locked up, trapped, incarcerated by our expectations? Are we not prisoners of our own hopes? Are we not inclined to confuse our particular points of view with God's purposes and assume that what we think best for everyone is exactly what God wants? None of us have much trouble justifying our own positions and identifying God with our expectations. Do not all of us claim to know how things ought to be, who has the right to rule, who is really deserving and who represents legitimate authority? We are "prisoners" of some pretty strange "hopes." And we don't need to ask for any confirmation or second opinion from either Yeltsin or Clinton or anyone else. For any leader knows, all too well, how fallible our human hopes, how fleeting fame, how fickle the crowds and how fine a line there is between supporter one day and detractor the next.

* * * * *

Which brings us to Judas. Let's think about him for a moment. He probably wasn't all that bad a guy, just a prisoner of his own false hopes and deeply disappointed when they weren't realized. Judas was probably a combination social reformer and political activist, a Zealot, who wanted to overthrow the Roman government. He wanted to see some changes in Jerusalem: the Roman choke-hold released and Israel rightfully restored—not unlike contemporary Zionist efforts. He was a "prisoner" who betrayed his leader only when Messianic hopes were dashed, when he found out that his great expectations for a new Jewish empire had evaporated into thin air. Jesus didn't fulfill Judas' hopes. So like many of us, Judas simply tried to salvage something from an otherwise bad situation. In many ways we're like Judas, who just didn't understand that any transformation of the world must ultimately come from within, any new kingdom—I mean radically new and different—will be—first and foremost—spiritual in nature.

Or, if we take offense at being compared to Judas, perhaps we'd prefer Peter. We all know that old, familiar story of Peter's denial three times before the cock crowed. Jesus had warned him that he too would fall away. NOT Peter. NO WAY. Of course, he didn't sell Jesus for 30 pieces of silver. NO, Peter resorted to the sword. He cut off the ear of Malchus. Standard human response when confronted with a crisis. Fight! That's always the street solution. Send in the Marines or a SWAT team. We must protect ourselves and defend our interests at all costs. I've had a number of occasions to talk with you about Peter this past year, so we are well aware that there's a lot of Peter in us just as there is a lot of Judas.

So the streets of Jerusalem were lined with "prisoners of hope" like Judas and Peter and, I dare say, the likes of you and me shouting "Hosannas" and singing "Hail to the Chief..." That's what we see on the surface and at the outset of Holy Week.

* * * * *

Of course, *THESE SAME PEOPLE WOULD CHANGE THEIR POSITION IN LESS THAN A WEEK. THE SAME PEOPLE WHO HAILED HIM ON SUNDAY, NAILED HIM ON FRIDAY!*

Does that offend anyone? Does it surprise anyone? It shouldn't! That's what happened. Not out of human character in the least. *THOSE WHO EXPRESSED AFFECTION ON PALM SUNDAY EXPRESSED REJECTION LATER IN THE WEEK.*

THOSE WHO HAD FOLLOWED FAITHFULLY THE MULTITUDE ON THE DAY WE ARE COMMEMORATING, ON GOOD FRIDAY FOLLOWED FEARFULLY, MAYBE OUT OF CURIOSITY, THE SAME MULTITUDE, UP THE VIA DOLOROSA, TO GOLGOTHA, THE PLACE OF THE SKULL NOT WANTING TO MISS A PUBLIC EXECUTION. A most popular form of entertainment in any age.

I wonder! No, honestly I don't wonder. We would have been there watching from the distance with the silent majority or watching it at home on the evening news. I think we can easily be identified in that crowd too. The Cinderella sandals of the multitudes anywhere slip on our human feet of clay all too comfortably.

So can there be any question in our minds who really qualifies for the "The Fickle Finger of *Faith*" award this week? Or, should I say, *Hope*? Those men and women who dramatically reversed themselves in less than a week's time. Perhaps we should make an example of them? Those terrible people who let it happen, even helped it happen and then watched it happen. Maybe we ought to get out all our hostility as if they were solely responsible for the tragedy. Heap all our scorn on them and make them scapegoats. Maybe that would make us feel better? As if there is nothing for us to learn about ourselves from Palm Sunday or the events of Holy Week.

You know Western Civilization has done that for centuries, namely, blamed the Jews as the Christ-Killers, saying, "Who could imagine such a terrible thing as they did?" We might think that we certainly would not have crucified our Lord, had we been there? And, frankly, I would hope that we would have acted differently. Otherwise, what difference does faith make or hope reflect if not in how we live and act! But such idealism needs to be tempered by a dose of realism. Deep human hatreds and ethnic loyalties and religious convictions and racial priorities that so divide and destroy persist all over the world in even greater strength and magnitude now than then. And despite all our disgust, we see evidence of the same reality in us too.

One of the most shocking moments in my life that took me to the epi-center of human reality and, simultaneously, to *The Encompassing Cross of Christ* was the day the Russians invaded Czechoslovakia. Years earlier I had entered college in 1957 with two Hungarian refugees, two students who had been throwing Molotov cocktails at Russian tanks in downtown Budapest while I was playing basketball. I soon became aware of their world and sensitized to what they had endured. Now it was over a decade later in graduate school and I had another Hungarian freedom fighter friend, this one was getting his Ph.D. in political science. The day of that fateful Czech invasion, I shared with him my heartfelt concern,

"I bet your heart goes out to Czech brother?" I said.

Do you know what his answer was? It absolutely devastated me. I will never forget it.

He looked me straight in the eye and said with cold dispassion, "No, I hope they kill all the sons-a-bitches!"

Does that offend anyone? It should offend us all, for it tells us something about ourselves? His response takes us past a lot of political correctness and polite rhetoric about who we are and lays bare human reality. It also takes us to the heart of Holy Week the Crucifixion. Yet even Christians treat Holy Week as if it's some—Yawn—"Ho-Hum" holiday? At best a vacation break, not something important to be taken seriously or—heaven help us—personally. We have so sanitized and sanctified the

Cross as to remove Palm Sunday and Holy Week from living reality.

* * * * *

Of the four gospel accounts of Palm Sunday the one we read from Luke I like best. It alone captures, for me, what Jesus perhaps felt or thought, the anguish and intense, internal struggle going on while all the hoopla was going on around him. People were dancing and playing—swishing and swatting each other with Palm Branches as if in some Finnish sauna—and his own disciples were leading the festivities. In Luke's account the Pharisees were especially upset by the disciples' conduct and the ease with which they identified Jesus with King David. But Jesus didn't reprimand his disciples. There was an atmosphere of *SILENT RESIGNATION* as if it was all out of his control? The scene was one of *MASSIVE MESSIANIC MISUNDER-STANDING:* pathetic, tragic, not in the least triumphant.

> "I tell you, if these were silent the very stones would cry out." (19:40)

He said painfully almost as if everything was stacked up against him on earth: heaven and nature in cahoots. Even his disciples, the very ones on whom the whole future depended, with whom he had spent so much time teaching and training, who should have known better, *MISSED THE POINT ENTIRELY, MISUNDERSTOOD THE MAN, AND MISCON-STRUED HIS MESSAGE.* Jesus' reply was one of despair. His life and ministry for naught....His own disciples encouraging the crowd. So His reply amounts to, "No, let 'em go. It's too late now." Everything He had worked for seemed lost. Perhaps his little explosion in the temple—chasing out the moneychangers—provided some temporary release. I find myself hoping He derived some small sense of satisfaction from expressing his frustration.

Luke was also the gospel writer who told of Jesus' response on entering Jerusalem. He indicated that when Jesus first caught sight of the city, "he wept over it, saying: 'Ah, if you only knew, even at this eleventh hour, on what your peace depends—but you cannot see it.'" (J.B. Phillips)

On entering the city, Jesus wept!—Real Messiahs don't cry! Not very heroic. Not very triumphant. No victory speech, no coronation, no inauguration. If we miss this point, I think we misunderstand Palm Sunday and miss the impact of Palm Sunday on our own lives. If we can't identify ourselves with the foolish disciples or the fickle crowds or even Jesus' frustrated response, in all likelihood we simply don't understand and probably misrepresent this man, (t)his ministry, (t)his message, and the meaning of this central week of Christian Faith. We can't afford to skip over lightly the intensity of Palm Sunday, or the similar trauma experienced in Gethsemane on Thursday and the end of it all on Good Friday and be able to fully appreciate EASTER. Easter does not stand out in isolation. We must stand with Jesus on this very day and see the world's mistake unfolding before our eyes—*MEGA MESSIANIC MISUNDER-STANDING*. We must retrace His steps as they impact our lives through the events of this week in order to fully appreciate God's transformation of foolishness into wisdom, fickleness into great faith, how the Cross itself, the symbol of hatred and cruelty and death, was transformed by God's love into genuine concern for one another in this world and compassionate acts and new life together. And, above all else, *HOPE* for all us prisoners.

So the important message of Palm Sunday tells us that the only truly triumphant entry is not a Messianic procession in some earthly city, but whenever God's transforming spirit of love enters human lives, penetrating our pretense, dispelling our hostilities, breaking down our resistance, bringing us real *HOPE*, by motivating us to live in harmony with one another, —a truly spiritual event, an experience of God within us.

So humbly and with hearts filled with *HOPE*, we enter this Holy Week seeking God's truly triumphant entry into our lives. We come again needing to be spiritually transformed: refocused, re-centered and renewed, for our humanity has been exposed this day. We await Easter with longing, for "Christ Jesus" is "our *HOPE*," (I Timothy 1:1). Christ in you—Christ in me—our *HOPE*..." (Colossians 1:27).

Let us pray...

Gracious God, we call to our minds this morning our Lord's 'triumphal' entry into a city representing a world that would reject Him. We ask for sufficient grace that we might welcome Him and serve him, when the truth is we too must confess our past welcomes have been like those He received in Jerusalem. We lay down palm branches, and sing "Hosannas" and say we believe. But our faith is skin deep. We know the superficial depths of our commitment; we know how far we would follow. More than likely we would have been in the same crowd that later crucified. Forgive us, we pray, and restore us to your continued service. Enrich our faith and enable us to follow all the way at least to the best of our ability, responsibly and faithfully. For Christ's sake, Amen.

PART III

– THE PRESENT –
LOVE and LIFE

THE LIFE OF LOVE

I Corinthians 13 concludes with that memorable last line: (that even if you haven't memorized the entire chapter yet, you already know at least this one line by heart).[1]

> "So faith, hope, love abide, these three. But the greatest of these is *LOVE*." (v. 13)

But that's not all Paul suggested. In the very next line I Corinthians, Chapter 14 begins with some great advice:

> "Make *LOVE* your *AIM*, and earnestly desire the spiritual gifts...." (14:1)

LOVE IS WHAT LIFE IS ALL ABOUT. LIFE IS LOVE IN ACTION. That is neither secret nor surprise. The AIM of LIFE for the Christian is to manifest as best we can in all our relationships and in everything we do, the *LOVE OF GOD IN JESUS CHRIST*. We don't always hit what we *AIM* at. Our *AIMS* for that matter aren't very good some times.

* * * * *

In these *TRI-VIA* sermons, at the center of the *cross-roads* as well as at the center of the *CROSS*, we see T*HE LOVE OF GOD IN JESUS CHRIST*, who as the author of Hebrews wrote,

> "is the same yesterday and today and forever." (13:8)

This sermon was delivered February 28, 1993, at First Federated Church, Peoria, Illinois. Scripture lessons were taken from Romans 13:8-10, I John 3:10-23; 4:7-12, 16-21 and II Thessalonians 2:16-17

The *CROSS* definitely *ENCOMPASSES* past and future, but we always find ourselves of necessity living in the present; right now and right here. In Christ it is always this day, today, that

"we live and move and have our being." (Acts 17:28)

From our present location here and now we can reflect backwards in time and project forwards and extend our influence elsewhere, but our experience is confined to present reality.

Of course, the present is constantly the past becoming the future. The present is at best a virtually indistinguishable point of transition from past to future. When does the past become the future, if not now? Even our own being is really always becoming. (It is somewhat gratifying to know we are all "has beens" of sorts who once were "somethings," but in the same breath we must be about what we can become.) It is always our potential to become better that is most important. And through it all it is the same *LOVE OF GOD IN JESUS CHRIST* that moves with us in this temporal process throughout our history influencing us and inspiring us, advising us, leading us...

To be Christ-centered and Love-oriented is not to suggest some static state of spiritual being. For the Christian the present is dynamic, because it is where the action is. It is also what has been called the "eternal present," the moment of eternity, "the eternal now."[2] To some extent we are limited to the present, but that limitation is eternal opportunity—right here and right now. The symbol of the *CROSS AT THAT CROSSROADS* both transcends time while it informs and motivates time-bound human "beings," who are always in the midst of transition. To quote Eve as she and Adam left the Garden of Eden, "Honey," she said, "we're entering a period of transition." (I didn't think that was all that funny either, but it was an interesting way of making my point.)

We are always in temporal transition, but with our unique ability as humans to transcend our present moments and encompass past and future. Our temporal experience and spiritual perspective influence how we think about everything.[3]

As was suggested in Part I:

The past is known in terms of *faith in Christ*, "the truth of faith."

The future, which was considered in Part II, is anticipated in terms of *hope in Christ*, "the way of hope."

And, thirdly, the focus of this morning, is the present, which we experience in terms of *love in Christ*, "the life of love."

So, once again, "faith, hope, love abide; these three; but the greatest of these is *HOW WE LIVE RIGHT NOW! HOW WE LOVE RIGHT NOW!*

Or, in the language of the Gospel according to John, where Jesus is recorded as having said,

> "I am the way, the truth and the life." (14:6)

THE WAY stretches out ahead of us in terms of the future.

THE TRUTH is already accomplished in an historical Christ-Event.

And *THE LIFE* is ALWAYS *LIVED* RIGHT NOW IN THE PRESENT.

When *LIFE is lived in LOVE*, on the one hand, we *demonstrate our FAITH*. Because it is on the basis of our present understanding of *faith* that we know *love is the way life is to be lived*, as we find in Galatians that beautiful phrase—

> "faith working through love." (5:6)

On the other hand, when *LIFE is lived in LOVE*, we *demonstrate our HOPE*. Because *faith* manifested in deeds of *love* both confirm God's presence and affirm God's purposes for the future. Moreover, when we *love* we help make *hope* happen for others.

* * * * *

LOVE IN ACTION summarizes the Christian *LIFE* which is always lived in a social arena, demonstrated in our relationships with one another in our respective communities. In

103

reflecting primarily on Chapters 1 and 5, I assumed, but neglected to state outright, that the entire enterprise is eminently *SOCIAL. FAITH, HOPE AND LOVE* have personal and individual elements, to be sure. But they are always demonstrated in the context of some human society and in a particular human community. There are no isolated individuals "living in love" based on the "truth of faith" and following the "way of hope"—ALONE. Even the hermit and the monk thought and prayed in a common language that was not uniquely theirs. You simply cannot love by yourself. To be human is to be *SOCIAL.*

Christian life is "the life of love" lived in a community, centered in that unique social setting called *the church*, because it is impossible *to love* and *to live* in isolation. And members of that special spiritual community are fellow travelers on the road or the *via*. Someone has suggested that Willie Nelson and I have at least one thing in common—we're both "On the Road Again."

Baptism puts us on that road or roadway or pathway that we travel together. That starting point also makes our Christian social life from the outset eminently *SACRAMENTAL* as well. In fact, the metaphor of *the way* becomes even more vivid if we pursue its Latin connections, for all along *the way*, there are little *vehicula*, the same word that gave us vehicle. These *vehicula* were intended to assist the traveler on the way, bear them, carry them, transport them like taxis, except they functioned more like little roadsigns. Because the Christian was expected to "walk in love"—a nice New Testament phrase (Romans 14:15, Ephesians 5:2). Christians were expected to walk together in love. And, of course, they were accountable for their behavior while walking. These sign posts served as little helpers to provide spiritual sustenance, to assist them and encourage them and remind them of their responsibilities, what we would call the "means of grace." Such things as prayer and the Bible and spiritual exercises and, especially, the Eucharist, functioned as a continual reminder of the *CROSS*. There *LIFE AND LOVE* met, "the truth of faith" remembered and the anticipated "way of hope" both realized in "the life of love" demonstrated there and practiced on the road. The symbols are all interrelated and converge at the center of the CROSS.

Moreover, our little time traveling spiritual community of saints, our little, earthly, social/sacramental tour group, includes all those that came before us and all those that will come after us, all centered and united in THE CROSS OF CHRIST, where those threeways converge. Perhaps all this is too neatly packaged for some and far too obscure for others? But it does provide a temporal and theological framework for us to think about some important Christian concepts as well as probe our personal experience in order to understand ourselves better spiritually.

Of course, our perennial problem with our lives lived in the present is how does one "LIVE IN LOVE?" What does it mean to live according to the CROSS OR THE CROSS-ROADS? What are we supposed to do? We want specifics! Are there absolute rules or does it depend on the situation, the context? Questions, questions, questions...

* * * * *

I have but three thoughts to suggest about LOVE that are not really answers to such questions at all. They at best point out "the way," without really telling us how to walk in it.

I. The first thought is from Jesus, who said in his Sermon on the Mount:

> "You have heard that it was said, 'An eye for an eye and a tooth for a tooth' But I say to you, Do not resist one who is evil....You have heard that it was said, 'You shall love your neighbor and hate your enemy.' But I say to you, Love your enemies and pray for those who persecute you;... for (GOD) makes (the) sun rise on the evil and on the good, and sends rain on the just and on the unjust. For if you love those who love you, what reward have you? Do not even the tax collectors do the same?

And if you salute only your brethren, what more are you doing than others? Do not even the Gentiles do the same? You, therefore, must be perfect, as your heavenly Father is perfect." (Matthew 5:43-48)

"Whatever you wish that men would do to you, do so to them; for this is the law and the prophets." (Matthew 7:12)

Actually, I prefer Luke's account.

"I say to you that hear, Love your enemies, do good to those who hate you, bless those who curse you, pray for those who abuse you. To him who strikes you on the cheek, offer the other also; and from him who takes away your coat, do not withhold even your shirt. Give to everyone who begs from you; and of him who takes away your goods do not ask them again. And as you wish that men would do to you, do so to them. "

"If you love those who love you, what credit is that to you? For even sinners do the same. And if you lend to those from whom you hope to receive, what credit is that to you? Even sinners lend to sinners, to receive as much again. But love your enemies, and do good, and lend expecting nothing in return; and your reward will be great, and you will be sons of the Most High; for (GOD) is kind to the ungrateful and the selfish. Be merciful, even as your Father is merciful." (Luke 6:27-36, cf. Leviticus 19:18, Proverbs 25:21-22, Romans 12:20)

Those passages alone are enough to discourage anyone from ever using the word *LOVE* again. We thought love was just being nice and polite and respectful and treating one another kindly, which is hard enough to do, even here at FFC. And then to learn that that doesn't even count, is too much for most of us. Does that mean now we have to listen to all those pre-recorded phone solicitations? How many times do I have to listen to AT&T and MCI messages? Does that mean owners of stores open twenty-four hours are supposed to let the same robber come back again and again?

No! Of course, not. But we get the message, don't we? We must think of Christian life and Christian love in new terms and press ourselves in our understanding and application of what it means to *LIVE IN LOVE*, because nice and polite and warm fuzzies are not good enough.

Reinhold Niebuhr (1892-1971) once called *LOVE* the "impossible possibility."[4] Indeed, *LOVE* is the "impossible possibility," especially, as exemplified in many of Jesus' statements, such as: "This is my commandment, that you love one another as I have loved you." (And we all know what that means and where it leads.)

> "Greater love has no (one) than this, that (we) lay down (our lives) for (our) friends." (15:13)

The *CROSS OF CHRIST* symbolizes and lifts up for us as an *AIM* worthy of our emulation, the ideal of *self-sacrificial love* as an "impossible possibility."

II. The second suggestion is that we are going to have to do more than just think about *LOVE*. As Christians we're obligated to do something, demonstrate love in deed, not just describe it, but transform our thoughts into acts, our words into deeds. Here I turn to the atheist Jean-Paul Sartre (1905-1980) for an excellent definition of *LOVE*, although that was hardly his intention. As in our Scripture readings from I John, Sartre helps us get beyond belief to conduct, beyond attitudes to actions, beyond the nebulous realm of ideas to actual involvement with the lives of other people. Wrote Sartre,

> "An individual life is the sum of one's deeds performed in a world of other people."[5]

That's it! *LIFE* is measured by our DEEDS DEMONSTRATED AND DONE IN RELATION TO OTHERS. To what extent our deeds are *LOVING* remains the haunting Christian question? And yet we as Christians proclaim the transforming power of God's love in a world shared with others—fully aware that God's *LOVE* acts like salt and light and leaven stirring, stimulating, transforming...

Why do we hesitate? Why do we resist doing what we know we should be doing? What are we waiting for? Some of you may remember Samuel Beckett's play, *Waiting for Godot*[6] In the end Godot does not come, but while "waiting for Godot," the characters in the drama relate to one another and share with each other the ragged coat, the shoes, the piece of turnip, etc. They are involved in one another's lives. What is illustrated is not the waiting, but the doing while waiting. Our opportunity—and the only opportunity we ever have—is in our given present moments, our right nows, just as in Beckett's play. There is the caring and the sharing and the sacrificing and the giving and the forgiving and always the patience and the courage it takes to love other people, who for the most part, are not very lovable.

The point is that the Christian needs to do more than look back in faith to what is believed true and more than look forward to the way ahead in terms of hope. And certainly *LIFE* is more than waiting. Life is doing, life is loving. The most important time—in fact, the only time the Christian has to act—is in the present time, where *FAITH AND HOPE ARE TRANSLATED INTO LOVE* which alone can transform *LIFE* and all our relationships.

III. Finally, as we enter Lent, a few words about the placement of the *CROSS* and the location of the *CROSS-ROADS*. Not that we do not have claim to the *CROSS* ourselves from our present location, nor that we are uninvolved at other *CROSS-ROADS OF LIFE*. Nevertheless, a statement of George Macleod of the Iona Community in Scotland always makes me rethink *THE ENCOMPASSING CROSS* and makes me uncomfortable. In my continuing attempt to share my discomfort, I conclude with his thoughts:

> "I simply argue that the Cross be raised again at the centre of the market place as well as on the steeple of the church. I am recovering the claim that Jesus was not crucified in a Cathedral between two candles, but on a Cross between two thieves; on the town garbage heap;

at a crossroad so cosmopolitan that they had to write his title in Hebrew and in Latin and in Greek (or shall we say in English, in Bantu and in Afrikaans?); at the kind of place where cynics talk smut, and thieves curse, and soldiers gamble. Because that is there He died. And that is what He died about. And that is where the church...should be and what the church...should be about."[7]

While we yet live, let us always *AIM* to love another better. And in all our present living be evermore loving and encompassing as demonstrated for us at the **CROSSROADS** in the **CROSS OF CHRIST.**

SPEAKING
THE TRUTH IN LOVE

This morning there is a single line from Micaiah, son of Imlah, or Micaiah ben Imlah, a *Prophet of Israel*, whose words leap from the printed page:

> "As the Lord lives, what the Lord says to me, that I will speak." (22:14)

The name Micaiah generally means "who is like Yahweh" or "who is like the Lord." It appears twelve times in the Old Testament, referring to both men and women, and is spelled three different ways. Micaiah Ben Imlah identifies our particular Micaiah du jour whose isolated appearance with King Ahab and King Jehoshophat ended with his prophecy against them coming true, which meant for Micaiah (for all we know) spending the rest of his life wasting away in prison, a popular prophet's reward.

Allow me first to recapitulate part of this intriguing story. We can visualize ole Micaiah standing up and speaking out courageously against 400 "court" prophets, the paid professionals, the "yes" men the king had hired to advise him. These 400 bureaucratic sycophants symbolize for us the herds of people today in politics or business or industry or the church or any other area—who always agree when their personal welfare is at

---

The idea for this sermon came from Reinhold Niebuhr (1892-1971) whose classes I enjoyed at Harvard Divinity School during the year he taught there (1961-62)[1] His sermon/essay, "Four Hundred to One," served as the starting point or stimulus. The present sermon was delivered July 22, 1990, at First Federated Church, Peoria, Illinois, with the Old Testament lesson taken from I Kings 22:128 and the New Testament lesson from Ephesians 4:11-5:2.

stake or a promotion or higher salary or job on the line. They always give in to easy conformity. I know, it's ethically nauseating, but that is what is called "the way of the world" and understood to be "the way to get ahead." Not so Micaiah! He went against the 400, and he went against the authority and power of two kings.

You see, the prophetic era began at the same time kingship did in Israel. When Israel developed a monarchy, it was accompanied by the institution of prophecy, a kind of check and balance system.

The prophets kept the kings honest.
The prophets reminded the kings of their role and responsibility.
The prophets represented the Lord and the Law.
The prophets were the mouthpiece of God, proclaiming God's truth.
All of which did not make the prophets very popular with kings and their courts.

Our story begins with a certain piece of property, Ramoth-Gilead, that is still contested today, that these two kings wanted. Ahab, in particular, because he was the real king; Jehoshophat was only his vassal. Ahab said the land rightfully belonged to them, so he tried to convince Jehoshophat to go to war against Syria for it. Jehoshophat probably didn't want to go, but had no choice since Ahab was the man in power. Jehoshophat hesitated, and as was customary, asked Ahab first to inquire of the prophets to see if it was the will of God. That's what the prophets were for. Ahab called a staff meeting of his cabinet prophets and all 400 advisors agreed. No surprise. They knew what Ahab wanted to hear, so they unanimously consented. In harmonious chorus they sang enthusiastically, "Of course, Ahab, go on up, for the Lord says 'you'll win.'" (22:6)

Maybe Jehoshophat suspected something, we don't really know. But he certainly wasn't satisfied, so he asked if there were any other prophets that should be consulted. "Couldn't we have a second opinion?" Ahab answered with a classic response, so keenly indicative of biblical insight into our human situation. Said Ahab, "Yes there is one other prophet of the Lord, Micaiah ben Imlah, but I hate him, for he never prophesies good concerning me, only evil." (22:8) Nevertheless, Ahab acquiesced and they decided to consult with Micaiah. One of Ahab's officers was sent to fetch Micaiah. The officer's remarks on finding Micaiah were equally classic and so utterly human. The typical party line, Little Sir-Echo-Messenger-of-the-King tells Micaiah to get with the program and cooperate. He said, "Micaiah, all the other prophets have agreed and they unanimously support the king, so, come on, don't you stir up things. Let your answer be like theirs and agree also." (22:13)

But our obscure, out-of-step, on another page, Micaiah, a rare individual with integrity, a representative of true prophecy, gave the king's messenger and all of us something to remember him by. His answer rings out across the ages against the tyranny of dishonest conformity wherever encountered.

> *"As the Lord lives, what the Lord says to me, that will I speak!"* (22:14)

What a man! I think, a truly great man. Like Luther, "Here I stand I can do no other."

But how do we differentiate between a true and a false prophet? Generally, the true prophet proclaims what we ought to hear, whereas the false prophet tells the people what they want to hear. But in the Micaiah story the distinction is complicated because the very Counsel of God placed a "lying spirit" among the court prophets in order to deceive the king.[2] Usually, we can tell the difference between true and false prophets by the consequences. As Micaiah told the king, "If you return in peace, Jahweh has not spoken" through me. Simple as that. Of course, Ahab didn't return. If we had read further, Ahab disguised himself in battle, but he was discovered and killed. He even had Jehoshophat decked out in full regal attire as a decoy, but the deception failed.

Any way we slice reality, it is hard to distinguish between truth and falsity. Perhaps Micaiah's solution is best as a standard test of prophetic truth. The proof is in the pudding; wait for the results, the consequences will not lie.

* * * * *

Now, given the complications and dangers inherent in prophetic witness and yet realizing the indispensability of standing up for what we believe and speaking the truth as we understand it, there are a few thoughts we might consider before we all rush out and hang up our prophet shingles.

1. First and foremost is commitment, commitment to Jesus Christ to the best of our all too fallible faith and limited ability as human beings, because there can be no prophetic Christian witness apart from a vital sense of the presence and purposes of God in and among us and in the world. But, in the same breath, we are all aware of widely divergent and conflicting Christian commitments with each variant claiming God's truth, sometimes exclusively and sometimes vociferously.

However, if we can't act on the basis of what we believe, then there is no point in believing or saying anything at all. We simply have to act on the basis of what we believe is the truth, the right and the good, and respond to what we believe God wants us to say and do. There is simply no way to circumvent the crucial and primary importance of Christian commitment (or at least some other form of commitment) aside from remaining completely uncommitted, which is a popular option. But as indispensable as Christian commitment is in some form, it hardly solves our problems.

We are all too familiar with serious conflicts between Christian people who are committed to various views of Christian truth and in good conscience. We are familiar with honest disagreement as a fact of everyday experience and certainly the church is no exception. Who can say that one person is committed and another not? Or, that one is speaking the truth and another not?

Some other means of measurement is necessary in order to determine whose prophetic truth claims we can accept and whose we have to reject, as each of us try to be true to ourselves and true to our God.

2. So a second prerequisite to think about in relation to prophetic witness is COMPASSION. Just as the prophets tried to keep the kings honest, compassion tends to keep our commitment honest. Once committed, the true test is compassion. Are we speaking the truth out of genuine concern for other people or because we have some unmet ego need? Prophecy has nothing whatsoever to do with what's in it for me! Prophets are concerned for people and speak the truth based on their understanding of God's love and justice. Here Paul helps us modify Micaiah. He puts "speaking the truth" into a Christian perspective for us when he adds the phrase "in love." Paul was talking about the whole church in terms of the human body and that "we are all members one of another." (Ephesians 4:24) In this setting, Paul wrote,

> "Rather speaking the truth in love, we are to grow up in
> every way into him who is the head, into Christ." (4:15)

So as an indication of our commitment to Christ, we are called to "speak the truth" prophetically, but qualified by the phrase "in love." Here is also a real clue to help distinguish between true and false prophets, and when we ought to speak out ourselves and when we ought to keep silent, a polite euphemism for "Shut up."

As Christians we care about the welfare of human beings, the quality of human life and how people are affected by our words and deeds. Speaking the truth in love does not mean, as some pop psychology suggests, 'tell-it-like-it-is-regardless-of-the consequences' or that the truth must hurt in order to be helpful, as if the more hurtful, the more helpful. Blatant honesty is not biblical prophecy and it is certainly not "speaking the truth in love." Blatant honesty is more a matter of personal catharsis or emotional release in order to allow the speaker to express his or her feelings by letting it all out without compassion.

Of course, "speaking the truth in love" can also hurt a lot. It can stir up controversy and expose pretense and deceit. We know that because most of us aren't all that interested in hearing the truth about ourselves revealed. So we should (by our own experience) be sensitized to how others feel. We have but to recall that truth put Micaiah in prison, or consider where God's truth revealed in Jesus Christ led Him—and how people reacted to that truth. The Encompassing Cross remains the central symbol and end result of prophecy and Jesus Christ's prophetic reward.

So even if we are practicing commitment tempered by compassion there is still great risk, especially when we superimpose our commitment and compassion on others. The history of Christianity contains some horrible examples of Christians committed to great causes and acting out of compassionate concern. Sometimes the most committed in the name of compassion can be the most dangerous and destructive. So even with these two prerequisites to consider, (commitment and compassion) there is no certainty as to when and where we should or should not stand up and speak the truth even in love.

3. That brings us to a third thought and that is COURAGE. In a way we've come full circle. In the end, even as modified Micaiahs, we have to act, we have to speak the truth in love in accordance with our commitment. To the best of our understanding and in accord with our conscience, each of us and all of us are left with how much we will risk for faith. All we can ask of anyone and of ourselves is that we act in good faith, do the best we can and with the courage of our convictions.

I have always found the voice and the vision of the prophets the most appealing aspect of the Bible and the church's witness through its long history. Men like Micaiah, Isaiah, Jeremiah excite the imagination and inspire us as they proclaimed the word of God in their particular historical situations.

In contrast, one of the most appalling aspects of the church in any period (and our own is hardly an exception) is when we have refused to proclaim the word of God and substituted something else; then our witness becomes pathetic rather than prophetic. When ministers are more concerned with who butters their bread than with what Jesus called "the bread of life," (John 6:35) we're in trouble.

Or, when Christians are more concerned with what is pleasing to parishioners and appeasing to opponents than with what probes the heart of faith and life.

Or, when congregations think the Christian life is just a matter of polite and respectable or acceptable habits that one can take or leave rather than doing responsible deeds in God's world and demonstrating God's love and justice.

It's the prophetic that concerns us, not the pathetic. it's the tragic triumphs of the true prophets, the unavoidable risks involved in any prophetic witness, which is to say the unavoidable risks involved in our trying to be faithful Christians, our trying to speak the truth in love, that reaffirms our faith, lifts our hope and energizes us to risk loving acts. I love the prophets for all their commitment and compassion and courage, and for all their controversy too. I am inspired and edified by their example. I admire them too for risking their lives, alien though such an idea is to us.

I'm not a prophet like Micaiah, though there may be some lurking aspiration. Today, consider the audacity of anyone saying, like the prophets did, "The word of God is specifically this and not that in any particular situation." Or, who of us would be bold enough to say, "Thus says the Lord..." with absolute certainty? Still with all these disclaimers and with some rudimentary awareness of the risks involved in prophetic Christian witness, nevertheless I want us to speak the truth in love to one another and to the world to the best of our ability. If there is one place in the whole world where you would expect people to speak the truth in love, it would be the church of Christ. And yet, ironically, many times the church is where you last of all look for it and least of all find it. But it doesn't have to be that way! We can be genuinely honest and compassionate and courageous within the framework of our faith. We can try to create that kind of prophetic atmosphere in our common life, saying and doing what we honestly believe God wants us to say and do, knowing at least some of the risks, but willing to take the risk of faith and release the rest to God.

I would hope that all of us here are sufficiently committed, compassionate and courageous to sustain a genuine prophetic Christian community, where we can all say with Micaiah,

> "As the Lord lives, what the Lord says to us, that will we speak."

And with Paul—"speak the truth in love" to one another and thereby experience more fully the spirit of the prophets and the spirit of Christ in our common life. In the context of the love of God let us celebrate "The Life of Love" we have received....

PRAYER OF THANKSGIVING

Gracious God, our Way and Truth and Life, we are grateful for the knowledge that You have been, will be and are with us in all times and places. We have experienced faith and felt the touch of Your love. We have known in our hearts Your presence as the source of our hope. We acknowledge that we always stand in need of greater faith, a more confident hope and the courage to love one another better. Help us in our common life to also acknowledge with astonishment the miracle wrought by 'works of faith,' 'labors of love,' and 'steadfast hope.' We marvel at Your work in us and among us and through us—to a world that needs to sense Your presence and purpose. The reality of Your Spirit, amazes us and moves us both to thanksgiving and service in and for the sake of our Lord Jesus Christ, whose kingdom we ever seek in our midst. Amen.

THE GOSPEL IN MINIATURE

For the last decade or so placards proclaiming "John 3:16" have appeared at major televised sporting events like Super Bowls, Golf and Tennis Tournaments, the World Series, the NBA Playoffs, the 1984 Olympics and the greatest sporting event of all that year, the 1984 Republican Convention. Early on, these unexpected John 3:16 signs popping up here and there seemed an innocent enough annoyance, but they quickly became irritating distractions. They were the product of a scene stealing, gallivanting, born-again Christian on the lunatic fringe and now on the lam. Presently, Rollen Stewart, alias "Rock 'n Rollen," more commonly known as the Rainbow Man— because of the outrageous tutti-frutti-colored wigs he wore—is wanted for a rash of stink bomb attacks and other explosive devices he allegedly set off at various sites in California including the Crystal Cathedral. He is now a fugitive wanted for various felonies and recently has proclaimed himself "the anti-Christ."[1]

Nothing, it seems, is sacred anymore! Even John 3:16, what Martin Luther once called "the gospel in miniature," is not exempt from exploitation.

Nearly everyone present this morning—even though memorization is currently out of vogue—could probably recite from memory this little 'nutshell gospel.' Because like motherhood and youth and infants, this single verse is a precious gem and most meaningful expression of our Christian faith:

This sermon was delivered May 10, 1992 at First Federated Church, Peoria, Illinois. Scripture lessons were taken from Numbers 21.4-9 and John 3:11-21.

"God so loved the world that he gave his only son that whoever believes in him should not perish but have eternal life."

I suppose it's the most widely learned of all Bible verses for Christians, because it speaks of *God's love* for us in Jesus Christ. And *love* is what is most frequently associated with our Christian faith. *Love* is what we like to hear about in church— or out of church as long as it is warm and comfortable. We don't like to trouble ourselves with 'tough love' or 'justice/love.' In fact, whenever we try to define love and pin it down to specifics, we can find ourselves getting uncomfortable. We prefer to leave it rather vague, or should we say, "open-ended."

Ironically, sometimes on Mothers' Day our love-talk can become so comfortable as to become really uncomfortable. No disrespect intended, but sentimentality and emotion can take over, and it all begins to sound like Mary Poppins—a spoonful of mother's love makes the medicine go down; the language is as syrupy as a bottle of Mrs. Butterworth's. Our gratitude and guilt combined can get a little gooey. I'm not challenging the significance of genuine mother's love which is indispensable. It's the *love and motherhood* and maple syrup connection that can be so s(t)ickeningly sweet your teeth rot as you read the greeting card messages.

Similarly, the unenlightened connection between *love and romance* can be equally obnoxious as if when romantic love strikes like lightening, lovers are swept away in whirling tornadoes of reverie and live happily ever after—to deliberately mix metaphors that were already mixed-up.

So just as a mother's love is a supposed panacea for every childhood ailment and social ill, and just as romantic love is proffered as the psychological cure-all for whatever ails adults, John 3:16 is frequently suggested as the religious solution for every spiritual problem of Christian life. All one needs to know about Christianity is God's LOVE-LOVE-LOVE...."How sweet the sound!"

But like motherhood and romance, our spiritual nugget this morning is not nearly as simple as it at first appears on the surface. And the love it speaks of is neither sentimental schmaltz nor s(t)ickeningly sweet. And, most important, the life faith offers and the relationship it describes is never easy nor glamorous.

If we really listen to this little verse carefully, it speaks of *THE CROSS OF CHRIST* as the Gift of God's Grace given in order to keep people from *perishing* or dying. And, that those who believe in God's love as manifested in Jesus Christ on the Cross will have...*life*. *John 3:16 is a passage about life and love in relation to death.*

Now we don't need to dwell at any length or depth on what it means to perish (which is to say, not to have life). Remove oxygen, remove water, remove food supply, vary the temperature ever so slightly, alter the delicate chemical balance, and life perishes. John is saying the lack of a healthy relationship with God is like shutting off our water, like closing the irrigation canals or drying up the wells in the desert and we human beings *perish* much like "the flower that fades" and the grass that withers, "surely, the people is grass," or so said the prophet Isaiah long long ago.[2]

The all important point we so often miss in this text is the connection between *the reality of God's love and real human life.* And that indispensable relationship is precisely what our "gospel in miniature" addresses.

Elsewhere in John there are numerous passages that speak of God *bringing life* to us in Christ. For example, in the sixth chapter we read:

> "For the bread of God is that which comes down from heaven and *gives life* to the world." (6:33)

Then Jesus identified himself as that

> "*bread of life*; he who comes to me shall not hunger, and he who believes in me shall never thirst." (6:35)

There are many passages like this—all packed with *life giving symbols of God's love.* In short, the message we get from the very first chapter of John and throughout the book is that *Jesus Christ was the source of new life for us;* and *that this life is what the love of God is all about.*

> "In Him was *life*, and the life was the light of everyone."
> (1:4)
>
> "The true light that *enlivens* every one." (1:9)

This is the Gospel of God's love, because the perennial problem for humanity is always the preservation of life in the face of inevitable death. John dealt primarily with this central human dilemma.

Now as we look at John 3:16 this morning, given its overuse and frequent misuse and its popularity, how can we bring new life—so to speak—to this pet passage? How can we think about it in a new way?

We must first put John 3:16 back into its proper Biblical context. More often than not, people pick it out as if it were a gemstone to be rescued from the mud or an isolated cashew from a can of mixed nuts. When, if we were really interested in understanding the verse and its message and meaning, we must see it in the light of those verses that surround it.

As you heard the passage read from the third chapter this morning, was there any question that stood out in your minds and demanded an answer? What strikes me as a major mystery in this chapter is the question, "What possible connection can there be between John 3:16 and all that Moses, Son of Man imagery and that snake stuff?" We skip over all that alien territory quickly on our way to that jewel of our faith, as if the rest were all archaic garbage or unimportant trivia—so much junk that impedes rather than enhances our understanding. And yet the meaning of John 3:16 is intimately related to this material and that wierd story we read earlier from Numbers about those snakes.

Listen again to the verse that precedes our text:

> "As Moses lifted up the serpent in the wilderness, so must the Son of Man be lifted up, that whoever believes in him may have eternal life."

This is the key verse that unlocks our understanding. The parallels between these two events, that Numbers snake story and our New Testament text, are truly amazing.

In the Numbers account all the Israelites were literally perishing from snake bite. They pleaded with Moses to seek forgiveness from God. So Moses prayed and was told to make a fiery serpent (probably of bronze) and to lift it up on a pole so that everyone could see it. Now the Old Testament doesn't say that the people who had been bitten were healed or cured or restored or got better. Rather that they looked upon the snake... *and lived...and lived....*

Similarly, in the New Testament, people were literally and spiritually perishing, lacking the means of genuine human life, so God sent Jesus, who was also lifted up on a pole, so that whoever believed in Him might...*live...or have life....*

The central parallel is clearly the *LIFE GIVING ACTIVITY OF GOD'S LOVE.* John is making a direct use of this outstanding passage in describing what God's love did in Jesus Christ for humanity; namely exactly what God had done for the ancient Israelite in the desert by means of Moses and the snake. *GOD GIVES LIFE. GOD IS THE GIVER OF LIFE! LIFE IS UNDERSTOOD IN RELATION TO GOD!*

Those who listened to John were probably familiar with Moses and would catch the connection that we sometimes, inadvertently, overlook. Moreover, for John even in death, *God's love gives life*; and that life begins when God's love is accepted by us and it lasts thereafter and ever after.

Elsewhere John wrote,

> "In this the love of God was made manifest among us,

that God sent his only son into the world, so that we might *live through him."* (I John 4:9.)

As Christians we believe *we have life, new life, even eternal life,* because of God's love for us. We believe that that love was self-sacrificial and once for all demonstrated in the crucifixion—the lifting up of the Son of Man on a pole. Belief in that event is the strange starting point of Christian Faith, and the beginning of Christian Life and the source of Christian Hope. But we've heard this many times, so many times before.

What remains even stranger about our passage is not that Jesus and Moses are compared or contrasted. That correlation is a familiar one whenever we consider the old covenant in relation to the new. Rather, what can be so confusing and complicated is when Jesus on the cross is compared to a bronze snake elevated on a pole. That seems like material for a Far Side cartoon. It almost seems idolatrous—at least in poor taste. What possible relationship could there be between Jesus and a snake? And, again, the answer involves *LIFE, our relationship with God and the love of GOD!*

* * * * *

Long before the Book of Numbers became a written document, those people who lived in Mesopotamia, between the Tigris and Euphrates Rivers, or present day Iraq, used the snake as an important and mysterious *SYMBOL OF LIFE.* In an ancient Babylonian story the tragic hero, named Gilgamesh, who was two-thirds god and one-third human, sought the secret of eternal life—so he traveled far and wide over the earth in search of some medicine of immortality (like Ponce de Leon in search of permanent youth). He had unimaginable adventures on his journey, like those of Homer's hero, Odysseus. Eventually, he came upon a certain Utnapishtim—who was all-god, not just two-thirds—who told Gilgamesh many things, (including a creation story and a flood story with many parallels to our Genesis stories). Finally, Utnapishtim, under great duress, told Gilgamesh that the secret of life—he said—"lies in a thorny plant at the bottom of the sea."

124

That tiny, thorny plant guaranteed eternal life. So Gilgamesh by tying heavy stones on his feet, according to the account, descended into the depths of the sea and obtained the plant which he named,

"MAN BECOMES YOUNG IN OLD AGE"

Gilgamesh had grasped the answer to our most perplexing human dilemma; he possessed the alternative to mortality—freedom from death. He held the *IMMORTALITY PLANT* in the palm of his hand.

Having succeeded in his quest, our elated hero began his long journey home. But, since he was one-third human, he soon became tired. Pausing at an oasis pool, he decided to take a dip and cool off. In so doing, he carelessly—humanly—left the tiny plant—the plant that held within it the secret of eternal life—on the bank unguarded, just for a few moments. While Gilgamesh skinny-dipped a snake came out of its hole, swallowed the plant and returned with its prize back into the mysterious earth. The snake had stolen from humanity the secret of life and had devoured it. A devastated Gilgamesh knew then, as the ancient epic concludes, that "when the gods created mankind, death (had not been) ...set aside."[3]

The moral of the story is that we humans must endure mortality. Ah, but that's not the whole story. This is not a lesson in herpetology or mythology, this is but background for our theological understanding of both Genesis and John. In the expulsion of humanity from the Garden of Eden, recall the central role a certain serpent played. Why were they expelled? Because a serpent had said, "Go ahead and eat of the fruit of the tree. You'll like it and God knows that when you eat of it, your eyes will be opened, and you will be like God, knowing good and evil."(Genesis 3:5) So God expelled them for their audacity and disobedience.... The verse concludes,

> "Lest they put forth their hands and take also of *the tree of life, and eat, and live forever.*"[4]

From this ancient near eastern story of Gilgamesh comes the idea that snakes possess eternal life. This belief was common property among the ancients and not necessarily restricted to Semitic peoples.

The *caduceus*, which comes from ancient Greece and serves as the symbol of the medical profession to this day, is related to this identification of the snake with the secret of life. You've seen the symbol, the two serpents entwined around the wand of Mercury. Mercury was the Greek messenger from the gods. And though the caduceus is identified with the healing arts, it is, nonetheless, the secret of life and God as giver of life that lies behind this medical symbol, and which accounts for the presence of the snakes entwined around the wand.

And so the use of a snake in the story from Numbers in all likelihood comes from a belief common to the ancient near east, which is directly related to the life-giving activity of the God of Israel. Much much later, the comparison was made in New Testament times between Jesus and the snake, in order to demonstrate continuity and illustrate the gift of life stemming from God's love as seen on the Cross of Christ. His love and life and death were seen as saving and healing, which is to say, *life giving in relation to God.*

We asked the parents of the children baptized this morning and then our confirmands, "Who is your Lord and Savior?" And so it would be good for us to ask ourselves again the same question, "Who is our Lord and Savior?" The word *Savior (soter swtnp)* means to heal as well as to save. Jesus as Savior and Jesus as Healer are synonymous. *To save* religiously—in Greek, *sozo*, and to heal physically or mentally, means the same thing; it means "to make *LIFE* whole" or complete in relation to God. The Bible is concerned about whole-life. Wholistic medicine and wholistic religion when fully cooperative best describe *WHOLE-LIFE.*

Jesus became known not only as the Lord and Savior in the early church but also as the Great Physician "of body and soul,"[5] touching persons with God's Love and making them whole in relation to God. God's love saves as it heals and heals as it saves, ever seeking to make whole body and soul, connecting the mental and the physical with the spiritual, which, again describes WHOLE LIFE. And in all this—mysteriously and symbolically—what connects the cross and the caduceus, Jesus Christ and Asclepius, is a snake, but a snake that connects religion and medicine that shares the same goals, for both at their best are centered on *LIFE in its WHOLENESS!*

On this Mothers' Day 1992 we have baptized infants and confirmed young people and celebrated the mystery of faith in which we live. We have looked upon the Cross on which Christ was lifted up as a symbol of God's love and life giving activity, even as a bronze snake had once been elevated on a pole in an ancient wilderness and even as today our modern medical community look upon the technological wonders of scientific accomplishment—all so that we might *LIVE* or "have *LIFE* abundantly" in all our relationships with God and one another.

> "For God so loved the world that He gave his only son on a cross that whosoever believes in him should not perish but have eternal life." (John 3:16)

Such is the mystery and the majesty and the meaning of our gospel in miniature. May God help us to so live ourselves and pass it on to others. May God help us to celebrate "the life of love."

"I said to my soul, be still, and wait without hope. For hope would be hope for the wrong thing; wait without love for love would be love for the wrong thing; there is yet faith. But the faith and the love and the hope are all in the waiting."

T.S. Eliot, *East Coker*
(1888-1965)

"Wait for the Lord and keep to the Lord"s way..."

(Psalm 37:34)

The trouble with the world is that "all we like sheep have gone astray; we have turned everyone to his own *way.*

(Isaiah 53:6)

"Make us to know Your Ways, O Lord; teach us Your Paths."

(Psalm 25:4)

EPILOGUE:
THE FINAL FORM OF LOVE...
FORGIVENESS

I remember entering The Menninger Foundation offices for the first time and picking up at the reception desk a little billfold-sized, promotion card. It had attracted my attention because on it was printed a favorite quotation from Reinhold Niebuhr (1862-1971), who had once been a professor of mine in seminary. The card read,

> "Nothing that is worth doing can be achieved in our lifetime; therefore we must be saved by *hope*.
>
> Nothing which is true or beautiful or good makes complete sense in any immediate context of history; therefore we must be saved by *faith*,
>
> Nothing we do, however virtuous, can be accomplished alone; therefore we must be saved by *love*."

Impressive though the quotation is as I just read it, the punch line—Niebuhr's most penetrating insight—was missing. I thought to myself, why had the conclusion been omitted? Because despite this beautiful expression of what we have been calling literally *TRI-VIA*, or the triumvirate of Christian virtues, I knew how the quotation was supposed to conclude.

> "No virtuous act is quite as virtuous from the standpoint of our friend or foe as it is from our standpoint.

This sermon was delivered March 14, 1993, at First Federated Church, Peoria, Illinois. Scripture lessons were taken from Mark 11:25-26, Luke 6:27-38; 7:37 38, 44-50, 23:34, Colossians 3:12 14.

Therefore we must be saved by the final form of love, which is *FORGIVENESS.*"[1]

So I asked Dr. Karl, why he hadn't included "the final form of love, which is forgiveness." He hesitated and then in his own inimitable manner changed the subject. I brought up the topic at least one other time. Again, he didn't want to talk about forgiveness. We need not jump to any unwarranted conclusions, especially those derived from silence.[2] Moreover, I am not inferring controversy, just alluding to a profound human dilemma. There is nothing human more unresolved and difficult, more mysterious or miraculous, given the healing that happens when it is occasionally practiced, than *FORGIVENESS.*

Most of us are not very forgiving. The way of the world is not forgiveness, the way of the world is revenge, getting even, giving to offenders—whatever the offense—whatever they've got coming to them, and probably more. An eye for an eye, a tooth for a tooth, (or better—maybe—two or three teeth for every one lost) one atrocity followed by a greater atrocity and further reciprocity—*lex talionis* followed by re-talionis ad infinitum.[3]

Actually, there are really two final forms of love. The other more familiar form is the supreme act of love as demonstrated at the very center of the *ENCOMPASSING CROSS OF CHRIST,* namely, *self-sacrifice.* This form of love was commended to us not only by the example of Jesus Christ and the crucifixion, but by his words:

> "This is my commandment, that you love one another as I have loved you. Greater love has no (one) than this, that (we) lay down (our lives) for (our) friends. You are my friends if you do what I command you." (John 15:12-14)

Though that generally defines and describes Christian love for us, still there is what Niebuhr called "the final form of love" that even puts our noblest self-sacrificial efforts into the humblest of perspectives. *FORGIVENESS!* As Jesus spoke from *THE CROSS:*

"Father, forgive them; for they know not what they do."
(Luke 23:34)

* * * * *

What does it mean to forgive?

I remember trying to understand forgiveness in terms of *acceptance*. Paul Tillich (1886-1965) once suggested that as God has accepted us for what we are, so we must accept others for what they are.[4] Does that help any of us understand forgiveness by instead reading acceptance? Does that mean we must accept—rather than reject—others regardless of what they might have done? Is blanket, carte blanche acceptance being commended here? Frankly, I find such an interpretation rather unrealistic. And yet, certainly, acceptance is an important part of forgiveness.

Then I remember trying to translate forgiveness into terms of *understanding*.[5] However, to try to understand what made someone do something, or to walk in their shoes, or to look at life from their perspective, while important, is also never the whole story. Does understanding mean that perpetrators are not accountable for their actions? So I "understand" them, so what? There has to be more to forgiveness than mere understanding.

Even if we say—following the example of Jesus—that we understand and that we accept the other person despite what they did, because they didn't know what they were doing, because they were stupid or ignorant or angry or couldn't contemplate the consequences of their actions, or think through the implications clearly...NOT UNLIKE ANY OF US AT LEAST SOME OF THE TIME?!

Or, one better, perhaps they were even sorry for what they hadn't intended to do and expressed regret, even though they had had no control over what tragically transpired. We can understand and we can accept the fact that they were not responsible for what happened and we can appreciate their remorse and willingness to make restitution when necessary. The results of their actions may have been devastating and the tragedy may have caused inordinate pain and irreparable damage, but there is also the element of compassion and mercy operative here. Though the whole idea of forgiveness causes me considerable discomfort and difficulty personally; nevertheless, I can go this far with **FORGIVENESS**.

I can even tolerate theological forgiveness of sin. Because I understand sin to mean essentially human nature. Sin comes with our being human. That's the way we are. We are all fallible, frail, fragile and filled with foibles. Consequently, we all stand in need of forgiveness, which is to say, **God's grace and mercy, God's acceptance and understanding**. We all have sinned or fallen short, or failed, or made mistakes. Our errors of omission and commission haunt us, because being human means we all have potential for good and evil and our efforts are realized in multifarious and always fallible combinations. All of us mess up. Sometimes even our little human mistakes can cause a lot of trouble. But, generally, with courage and compassion we can excuse or forgive one another, insofar as the sins were trivial in the normal, inconsequential sense of the term. And insofar as they were not done with deliberation. That adds a different dimension to our discussion. It's the bigger messes that we do deliberately and deceitfully and hurtfully—for which we are also responsible—that cause the greatest grief and demonstrate how unforgiving we all are. And how "Unforgiven" many should remain—Clint Eastwood included.

But before considering why I think genuine human forgiveness is simultaneously virtually impossible and absolutely indispensable, there are a number of other complications that enter into our discussions of FORGIVENESS that at least warrant mentioning:

(I) First, whereas it's one thing to forgive others, it is quite another thing to forgive ourselves. Sometimes it's easier to forgive others than to forgive ourselves. It's hard for some of us to admit error and even harder then to do something about it, namely, to change our ways.

But there are those, on the one hand, who cannot and will not admit that they ever do, did or done wrong. Sounds like a good Country/Western song.

At the other extreme are those who in desperation acknowledge wrongdoing. They are so overwhelmed by the evil that they did that they are totally incapable. The evil cannot be erased or ever eradicated. Not only is the done deed beyond forgiveness, as doers of the deed he or she or they are unforgivable. Such views can lead to suicide. Or, they can be used to justify further deplorable and despicable acts.

I should point out here that the current language of self-acceptance and self-understanding and self-esteem can take on new meaning given this context. But the point in mentioning this first concern is to put the question personally and directly to each of us. "Are there conditions for which no forgiveness is possible?" "Are there certain deeds, that if we did them, we could never forgive ourselves?" I suggest there are.

(II) A second complication takes us beyond our ability or inability to forgive ourselves and back to our understanding and acceptance of others' behaviors, which is an entirely different matter. How much difference can we tolerate? Or, to use the current jargon word—*diversity*—better yet, *multi-cultural diversity*. Diversity and democracy that ideally go together can depict either the creative edge of culture or point to its catastrophic conclusion. *The tests for any true democracy are the limits of its tolerance.*

Translated: how much diversity can we tolerate without destroying ourselves?

Beirut was once the marvelous hope of a diverse world with Muslim, Jew and Christian communities all living there together in "tolerable harmony," another neat Niebuhrian phrase.

Similarly, Sarajevo once exemplified the idealism of diversity. Now given Balkan reality Marshal Tito (1892-1980) suddenly seems like an unheralded hero. Is it better to control by fiat or fear ethnic inability to tolerate diversity? Or, in the interests of human freedom or fate, should the controls be released and centuries of pent up vengeance unleashed?

Rebecca West (1892-1983) wrote a book in 1942[6] which could be summarized by one of her lines, "Violence was, indeed, all I knew of the Balkans...," she wrote. That was fifty years ago. She described a region that had never known peace, only mutual destruction and hatred and annihilation, centuries of violence and vengeance.

Of course, the democratic experiment we know as the United States of America remains the hope of the world when it comes to tolerating diversity. How tolerant are we? How tolerant should we be?[7]

(III) Then, thirdly, there is this matter of *responsibility*.

I cannot stand here and say to those Bosnian women so horribly brutalized, "Forgive those who raped you; bless your captors."

"Pray for those who abuse you." (Luke 6:28)

I cannot say to the families of anyone murdered anywhere, "You have to understand and accept the situation of the murderer."

After spending most of my life involved in caring for abused and abandoned children, can I say to the children—as our state and federal policies require us to do—"Your mommy and daddy really love you and we'll try to get you back home as soon as we can." I couldn't say that to many children anyhow, whose lives have been snuffed out by their mommies and daddies.

All of us are responsible for our behavior and fully accountable for the consequences of our actions. But given the irresponsible human way of the world, is there any *hope* for us? Is there anything that can save us from our literally *atrocious* existence?

* * * * *

134

Before attempting a response to such questions, there is one more atrocious illustration that for me provides the critical context from which these thoughts first emerged. I read a quotation someplace attributed to Adolf Hitler (1889-1945) to the effect that the world didn't pay any attention to the Turks annihilating well over a million and a half Armenians, so who would miss a few Jews? I've been trying to locate that quotation for sometime now, albeit unsuccessfully thus far. However, I did find another involving the Armenians, whose plight I want to bring before us anyhow. And it makes the same point.

Prior to Hitler's Polish invasion in 1938-1939, he prefaced an order as follows:

> "Our strength consists in our speed and in our brutality. Genghis Khan led millions of women and children to slaughter—with premeditation and a happy heart. History sees in him solely the founder of a state. It's a matter of indifference to me what a weak Western European civilization will say about me."

> "I have issued the command—and I'll have anybody who utters but one word of criticism executed by a firing squad—that our war aim does not consist in reaching certain lines, but in the physical destruction of the enemy. Accordingly, I have placed my deathhead formations (namely, his SS military organization) in readiness—for the present only in the East—with orders to them to send to death mercilessly and without compassion, men, women and children of Polish derivation and language. Only thus shall we gain the living space (*Lebensraum*) which we need. Who, after all, speaks today of the annihilation of the Armenians?"[8]

Most people today know nothing of Armenia or its history. The holocaust has caused us all but to forget the Armenian massacre that preceded it. And yet as we just read, the world's lack of concern for Armenia made Hitler's atrocities possible. Why Armenia? Because I had my own moral abhorrence to violence awakened as a child, when I read about the atrocities that in particular began about a hundred years ago and culminated during World War I with over a million lives destroyed, a modern example of the term *genocide* before it was officially coined.[9] Today Armenia remains essentially a Christian nation despite being in the old Soviet bloc and surrounded almost entirely by Muslim nations. I know the current war with Azerbaijan over Nagorno-Karabakh is presently dwarfed by greater catastrophes even in that very region, such as the plight of the Kurds not that far away.

I selected Armenia because of Hitler's unforgivable inexcusable use of Armenian atrocities to legitimate his own atrocities.

I selected Armenia because of persistent Turkish and Muslim denial to this day that anything ever happened for which they were **responsible**.

I selected Armenia because it reminds me of Bosnia reversed.

Of course, if we weren't mostly white and western and Christian, we could have cited other locations of past memory and present reality equally unforgivable, such as this week's atrocities in Natal or as exposed in El Salvador. Ultimately, the place is of less importance than the people responsible for making this world a killing field (whether there are any oil fields there or not).

* * * * *

Is there any hope for our world? Any evidence of that "final form of love, which is forgiveness" that alone might save the world? Allow me to lift up a tiny example as a little candle struggling to stay alight in the cold wind of the world's dark night. It stands like our *ENCOMPASSING CROSS OF CHRIST*, at best a spiritual symbol of promise and inspiration.

In John Calvin's Genevan theocracy, there was a heresy trial. In anger John Calvin had his bitter opponent, a brilliant young theologian Michael Servetus (1511-1553) bound to a stake with two of his books tied to his waist and a crown of straw and brimstone placed on his head and burned to death before his friends and enemies alike on October 27, 1553.[10] A minor atrocity we would say, almost negligible today in a world of such massive atrocities. Nevertheless, a blemish, a blight on the Reformer, his church and the community.

Three hundred and fifty six years later, on the anniversary of his death in the suburb of Champel at an angle formed by the crossing of two unfrequented roads, the citizens of Geneva erected a monument to commemorate this single incident in their history that had so blotted their good name. I visited the monument in 1976. One of the streets is now named Rue Servet. There it was—a rough, irregular granite block about a man's height resting on a natural stone base. On one side, the name of Michael Servetus, and on the other the following inscription translated from French:

> "With all due respect and gratitude for Calvin our great reformer, Servetus was condemned for an error which was peculiar to his century, one who firmly adhered to the liberty of conscience according to the true principles of the Reformation and the Gospel, we have built this monument as an act of atonement." (or we might even say, as an act of expiation or as a sin offering…)[11]

In that tiny but significant acknowledgement to the world that their ancestors had been wrong and that they wanted to make amends is found a tiny ray of hope. They were sorry and they hoped the world would understand and accept their act of repentance. It's so minuscule given the magnitude of modern atrocities that we are amazed. For neither the Turks nor the Germans nor the Russians nor the Japanese nor the Khymer Rouge nor the British nor the IRA nor the Israeli nor the USA can seem to accept any responsibility and repent. When have you heard of a nation asking the rest of the world for forgiveness? Or, a politician of his colleagues or opponents? In this isolated instance is the spiritual spark of conscience, compassion and concern that comes from *FAITH* and brings us *HOPE*. In that tiny flame of forgiveness is the message of God's *LOVE* emanating from the Center of the Cross, "the final form of love" that alone can save the world from itself. *FORGIVENESS* takes us to the heart and hurt of God's *LOVE* at any *CROSS-ROADS* of life.

But then, just when we think we're beginning to see some light at the end of that long tunnel, we are reminded of the Gospel. Here we are mortals murmuring about our pettiness that constitutes most of our forgiveness among friends, which is hard enough for us to accomplish. And then Jesus tells us,

> "You have heard that it was said, 'You shall love your neighbor and hate your enemy.' But I say to you, Love your enemies and pray for those who persecute you....For if you love those who love you, what good is that?" (Matthew 5:43-44, 46)

And the Apostle Paul likewise:

> "Bless those who persecute you; bless and do not curse them....Repay no one evil for evil, but take thought for what is noble in the sight of all. If possible, so far as it depends upon you, live peaceably with all. Beloved, never avenge yourselves, but give place to the wrath of God; for it is written, 'Vengeance is mine, I will repay, says the Lord.' No, if your enemy is hungry, feed him; if he is thirsty, give him drink....Do not be overcome by evil, but overcome evil with good." [12]

Here we are living in a world filled with unforgiving people bent on revenge and mutual destruction. And God's response is to give us the *CROSS! THE ENCOMPASSING CROSS* is our central spiritual symbol for creating a better world contingent upon our response to this love answer—this impossible possibility—this *FORGIVENESS AS THE FINAL SOLUTION—THE MOST IMPOSSIBLE OF ALL POSSIBILITIES!*

God's offer of hope for our world hasn't worked thus far, though it has never really been tried. *FORGIVENESS* not only of our friends, but especially our unforgivable enemies. *FOR-GIVENESS* is not a little, inadvertent, unimportant spiritual suggestion. *FORGIVENESS* is not God's good idea, but not to be taken seriously. *FORGIVENESS* is a necessity—our only possibility for transforming and mending and making whole a world in pieces by first transforming people like you and me by the final form of love, which is *FORGIVENESS!*

Gracious God, forgive us all, for none of us ever really know what we do. And help us ever not to be overcome by evil or vengeance, but to overcome evil with good....

PERSONAL NOTES AND RESOURCES

INTRODUCTION:
THE ENCOMPASSING CROSS
—A MATTER OF FAITH

1. *The Melody of Theology—a Philosophical Dictionary* Cambridge: Harvard University Press, 1988, p. 88.
2. *The American Behavioral Scientist* 6, 1963, pp. 58-60.
3. Introduction by Carl Sagan, Toronto: Bantam Books, 1988. There is even a companion workbook that can be purchased.
4. Painted in 1931. Dali was quoted in 1968, "The specialized sciences of our times are concentrating on the study of the three constants of life: the sexual instinct, the sentiment of death, and the anguish of space-time." *Dali* Introduced by J. G. Ballard, edited by David Larkin, New York: Ballantine Books, 1974.
5. *Irish Literature* Volume IX, Philadelphia: J.D. Morris & Company, 1904, p. 3389.

CHAPTER I
THE TRUTH OF FAITH

1. Subtitled *Introduction to a Metaphysic of Hope* translated by Emma Craufurd, New York: Harper & Row, Torchbook edition, 1962.
2. I should add that "The Ten Commandments" were used as the focus of our concurrent Lenten Wednesday evening programs.
3. A volume written by James Muilenburg, New York: Harper & Brothers, 1961.
4. Matthew 22:16, cf. Luke. 20:21, Romans 11:33.
5. Dag Hammarskjöld, *Markings* New York: Alfred A Knopf, 1964. See further *Dag Hammarskjöld's White Book—The Meaning of Markings* by Gustaf Aulen, Philadelphia: Fortress Press, 1969.
6. I recall reading a number of years ago a delightful little book of meditations for the Lenten Season by Willard Sperry, *Those of the Way* New York: Harper and Brothers, 1945, well worth anyone's reading, if the volume can be located.
7. In John there are a number of self-designating and descriptive "I am…" statements such as "I am the bread of life," (6:34) "I am the Good Shepherd," (10:11) "I am the true vine," (15:1) or "I am the light of life." (8:12) For starters, see "Christological Perspectives in the Predicates of the Johannine *Ego Eimi* Sayings," by Harvey K. McArthur in *Christological Perspectives* edited by Robert F. Berkey and Sarah A. Edwards, New York: Pilgrim Press, 1982, pp. 79-94.

CHAPTER II
FIRST HAND FAITH

1. These poems are both from e e cummings (1894-1962). The first is from *Xaipe*; the second was quoted and used as the frontpiece in Harry and Bonaro Overstreet's *The Mind Alive* New York: W.W. Norton & Co., 1954.

2. Phillips Brooks (1835-1893), a famous Episcopalian bishop, was asked by Helen Keller's father to help her understand faith. Using the language of his day, Bishop Brooks introduced her to the idea of God's love by telling her about the fatherhood of God and the brotherhood of man. She delighted him one day when she told him, "I knew all about God before you told me, only I didn't know His name." He wrote to her from London, "Let me tell you how it seems to me that we come to know about the Heavenly Father. It is from the power of love which is in our hearts. Love is the soul of everything. Whoever has not the power of loving must have a very dreary life indeed.... All the love that is in our hearts comes from Him, as all the light which is in the flowers comes from the sun; and the more we love the more near we are to God and His love....I love to tell you about God, but (God) will tell you Himself by the love which He will put into your heart if you ask Him....And so love is everything; and if anybody asks you, or if you ask yourself what God is, answer 'God is love!'" Raymond W. Albright, *Focus on Infinity—A Life of Phillips Brooks* New York: Macmillan, 1961, pp. 349, 351f.

3. We cannot forget Augustine's mother, Monica—technically Monnica—a devout Christian woman, who greatly influenced Augustine. During one of Augustine's many pre-Christian excursions, his mother had a dream in which her son stood beside her and said, "Where you are, I am." She lived to see that dream realized. For "A Sketch of the Life and Character of St. Augustine," see C.C. Martindale, S.J. *A Monument to Saint Augustine—Essays on Some Aspects of His Thought Written in Commemoration of His 15th Centenary* London: Sheed & Ward, 1945, pp. 81-101, and "The Life of St. Augustine" in *A Companion to the Study of St. Auaustine* edited by Roy W. Battenhouse, New York: Oxford University Press, 1955, pp. 15-56. These introductions and others available should not replace the importance of exploring St. Augustine's *Confessions*.

4. There are many great books on Luther available. I commend to your attention *Luther—His Life and Times* by Richard Friedenthal, translated by John Nowell, New York: Harcourt Brace Jovanovich, 1970, and Heiko A. Oberman, *Luther—Man between God and the Devil*, translated by Eileen Walliser-Schwarzbart, New Haven: Yale University Press, 1989. Luther's *Lectures on Romans* should be consulted as translated and edited by Wilhelm Pauck, The Library of Christian Classics XV, Philadelphia: The Westminster Press, 1961.

5. There are many biographies of John Wesley. The one I recall reading and from which most of the citations come is *The Life of John Wesley* by C.T.

Winchester, New York: The Macmillan Company, 1922. However, the first biographical sketch I recall reading was written by Ralph S. Cushman. I have long since misplaced the volume. The reader may also be interested in Edgar Legare Pennington's article, "John Wesley's Georgia Ministry," *Church History* 8 (September, 1939), pp. 231-254.

6. Winchester, p. 52.
7. Cushman, p. 96.

CHAPTER III
ON FIRE INSIDE

1. This delightful offering is quoted with permission of its author, J. Carter Swaim (1904-   ). It can be sung to the hymn tune *Truro*. Dr. Swaim is a pastor, Biblical scholar, contributor of 109 articles to *The Interpreter's Dictionary of the Bible*, former professor of New Testament Literature and Exegesis at Western (now) Pittsburgh Theological Seminary and author of a number of books including, *Do You Understand the Bible* Philadelphia: Westminster Press, 1954, and *The Book God Made—The Story of the Holy Bible* New York: Hawthorne, 1959, published while he was Executive Director of the Department of The English Bible, National Council of Churches, 1954-1964. One of his recent contributions is *War, Peace and the Bible* Maryknoll, New York: Orbis Books, 1982.

2. Emil Brunner (1889-1966). Among the books of this Swiss theologian are *The Mediator* tr. 1934, *The Divine Imperative* tr. 1937 and his Gifford Lectures of 1947-48, 1948-49 entitled *Christianity and Civilization*. See especially, *Faith, Hope and Love* Philadelphia: Westminster Press, 1956.

3. *Explanatory Notes Upon the New Testament,* John Wesley, New York: Lane & Tippett, 1847, comments on Luke 24:32, p. 208.

4. Jeremiah 31:33., cf. Luke. 22:20, I Corinthians 11:25. The logical and traditional way for us to conclude would be to lift out of Jeremiah a message of hope and end on that note, not dwell on divine discontent and disturbing love. There is certainly evidence of hope in Jeremiah. Some have even seen in Jeremiah a "book of hope" (e.g. 31:3, 38; 29:13-14) There is even hope beyond what Jeremiah knew in the new covenant he prophesied, which as Christians we know—the hope that lies on the other side of the tragic cross. But there is no need for short-cuts or skipping over lightly the reality that confronted Jeremiah in his day and that which confronts us in our day.

5. See Jeremiah 6:25; 20:3; 46:5; 49:29.

6. Jeremiah 11:18-23; 12:1-6; 15:10-12, 15-21; 17:12-18; 18:18-23; 20:7-18.

7. Cf. Jesus' sorrows, Mark 14:33.

8. Cf. Exodus 22:16, I Kings 22:19-23.

9. Isaiah 6:6-7, cf. Amos 3:8, I Corinthians 9:16.

CHAPTER IV
LEAPING FORWARD FAITHFULLY

1. His practice of dating events from the time of the Incarnation led to our practice of making B.C.—A.D. distinctions.
2. The error continues but at a rate of 3 days every 400 years, so 3 of every 4 centesimal years ending in 00 were made common years not leap years. The year 1600 was a leap year, and 2000 will be a leap year. Leap years are divisible by 4 except centesimal years, which are common unless divisible by 400. For scientific accuracy and a more adequate explanation, consult encyclopedic resources.
3. New York: Harcourt, 1952, pp. 145f., as quoted by Conrad Massa, "Truth," *Princeton Seminary Bulletin* LVI (3), May, 1963, p. 40.
4. See *Concluding Unscientific Postscript* translated by David F. Swenson and completed by Walter Lowrie. Princeton: Princeton University Press, 1941, pp. 178-182. There are many insights in Kierkegaard's "teleological suspension of the ethical" and his "knight of faith." His definition of truth follows:

   "*An objective uncertainty held fast in an appropriation-process of the most passionate inwardness is the truth,* the highest truth attainable for an *existing* individual....The truth is precisely the venture which chooses an objective uncertainty with the passion of the infinite...."

   "But the above definition of truth is an equivalent expresson for faith. Without risk there is no faith. Faith is precisely the contradiction between the infinite passion of the individual's inwardness and the objective uncertainty." Ibid.
5. Here the parallelism between Yahweh and Yerah could be expanded.
6. "The Will to Believe," *Essays in Faith and Morals* selected by R.B. Perry, Cleveland: World Publishing Co., 1967, pp. 28, 96.
7. Ibid., p. 62.
8. See further, *To Know as We are Known* New York: Harper & Row, 1983, p. 31. Palmer goes on to talk about a community of troth as in a congregation—an interesting idea—equally applicable to the educational community.

CHAPTER V
THE WAY OF HOPE

1. Alexander Pope (1688-1744) *An Essay on Man* Epistle 1. 95.
2. Acts 23:6, 26:6; I Thessalonians 4:13; I Peter 1:3; I John 3:3; I Corinthians 15:19.
3. Or, (5) we could talk in more traditional terms in the language of the *hope of salvation,* or (6) the *hope of the triumphant Second Coming* (Titus 2·13, I

Peter 1:13; I John 3:3) or, again, in the language of the Bible, (7) *the hope which is laid up for us in heaven*. (Colossians 1:5)

4. I can recall the book that changed significantly the way I thought about predestination. After reading Aquinas and Calvin and other old standards, I read Pierre Maury, *Predestination & Other Papers* Richmond: John Knox Press, 1960. Should the volume be available I commend it to you.

CHAPTER VI
"LOOKING BACKWARD" HOPEFULLY

1. As will become evident the sermon title and theme is from Edward Bellamy, *Looking Backward 2000-1887* New York: Grosset & Dunlap, n.d., originally published in 1887 by Ticknor and Company, pp. xix, 10-13. Bellamy was a journalist and a social reformer. Because of his efforts the Nationalist Party was formed and the magazine *The New Nation* created. I first read this book probably in 1962, and previously had preached a sermon based on it in 1973 using Genesis 19:15-26 and Luke 17:32-33 and Luke 9:57-62, cf. I Corinthians 9:10 as texts.

2. "Child," by W.L. Stidger, as quoted in *A Little Girl is Something to Love* edited by James L. Murat, Stevens Point, Wisconsin: The Makepeace Colony Press, 1967, p.7. William Stidger was a pastor whose ideas have been most helpful to me, first as the pastor who suggested writing "Thanksgiving Letters"—as a special way to celebrate the month of Thanksgivings, namely, November. He set aside a portion of each day to write a letter of thanksgiving to someone who had made a difference in his life. What a great idea. He was also the author of a biography I especially appreciated. See *Edwin Markham* New York: Abingdon, 1933.

3. Sainted by the Roman Catholic Church as he was beheaded for refusing to recognize Henry VIII as the head of the Church of England. More assigned the narrative to a Raphael Hythloday—Greek for "talker of nonsense." The book was written in Latin and not translated into English until 1551. More was executed in 1535.

4. See entry under "evangelist" in Joseph Shipley, *Dictionary of Word Origins* New York: Philosophical Library, 1945, p. 144.

5. *Thesaurus of Book Digests* compiled by Hiram Haydn & Edmund Fuller, New York: Crown Publishers, 1949, pp. 239-240 .

6. His autobiographical novel, *The Way of All Flesh* (1903) is considered his masterpiece. Cf. Rudyard Kipling's "Recessional" in relation to the dissolution of the English Empire.

7. He wrote the book less than two years after the great labor struggles of 1886. Immediately following his success, other writers wrote a raft of utopian novels, some with such "creative" titles as *Looking Further Backward* (A.D. Vinton) and *Looking Further Forward* (Robert Michaelis).

8. The use of Jeremy Bentham's (1748-1832) phrase as a self-evident principle of utilitarian morality is intended not as a panacea, but as a paradigmatic possibility.

9. Cf. Luke 8:18; 19:26.

10. As quoted by Rollo May, *Man's Search for Himself* New York: W.W. Norton, 1953, pp. 276-277.

CHAPTER VII
THE HOPE OF THE WORLD

This sermon was first preached at First Presbyterian Church in Topeka, Kansas, early in 1977. Thereafter I used it as a basis for numerous sermons, keynote addresses and church programs related to the work of The Villages, Inc., and Child Advocacy Programs, such as the keynote for "Advocacy: The Child and the Church" an event sponsored by the Synods of Mid-America, United Presbyterian Church U.S.A. held at St. Paul School of Theology, Kansas City, Missouri, September 29-30, 1981. It also appeared in another form as the epilogue in *Sacred Shelters—Church Related Children's Homes* which presented some of the papers presented at Wingspread Conference on The Church and Residential Child Care held in Racine, Wisconsin, November 5-7, 1980. The title and text was used as framework for introducing various themes, such as the development of group homes, addressing teenage pregnancies and other issues pertaining to the church and the care of children.

1. I hope I have represented Mr. Buckles' address and intentions adequately. The essence of his speech was conveyed to me by those who heard him.

2. See Robin Marantz Henig, "For Many, Pediatric Neurosurgeon Is a Folk Hero," SCIENTIST AT WORK—BENJAMIN S. CARSON, *New York Times*, Tuesday, June 8, 1993, Section B, pp. 7, 10.

3. The passage is also a significant point of departure for those interested in understanding the role of prophecy in the New Testament.

4. Hans-Ruedi Weber has pointed out that the Latin verb "to lift up" *suscipere* became a synonym for survival. See *Jesus and the Children—Biblical Resources for Study and Preaching* Atlanta: John Knox Press, 1979, pp. 6-8, 65-66.

5. Prior to a decade of creating family group homes and administering programs for abused and abandoned children with The Villages, Inc. primarily in Kansas and Indiana, in the sixties with a number of churches we started Steel Valley Homes for Youth in Youngstown, Ohio. Then in California our congregation started a home for girls and then an emergency shelter home. Most of the homes for children in the United States, if not operated by churches, originated in churches.

6. Quentin Rae-Grant, "Economics of Theory and Therapy in the Treatment of Children, as reported by Perihan Aral Rosenthal in "Summary Reports" 57th Annual Meeting, Toronto, Ontario, April 7-11, 1980, p. 9.

7. Printed with permission of Ina Hughs, *A Sense of Human* Knoxville: Knoxville News-Sentinel, 1993.

CHAPTER VIII
PRISONERS OF HOPE

CHAPTER IX
THE LIFE OF LOVE

1. The weeks when these TRI-VIA sermons were delivered and thereafter throughout Lent, the congregation of First Federated Church was encouraged to learn I Corinthians 13. Portions of the worship service each Sunday were devoted to "practice."

2. Here I am reminded of a book of sermons by Paul Tillich (1886-1965) entitled *The Eternal Now* New York: Charles Scribner's Sons, 1963, an underlying theme in his theology. Moreover, I am aware of the influence of Christian existentialistic thought in general. More recently this theme was prominent in the thinking and writing of Joseph Campbell (1904-1987). I am thinking in particular of references to "eternity" found in his book *The Power of Myth with Bill Moyers*, edited by Betty Sue Flowers, New York: Doubleday, 1988.

3. This is a good example of the "Forms" or "Intuitions" of "Sensibility" developed by Immanuel Kant (1724-1804). All thinking and whatever we claim as knowledge is conditioned by these two "Forms" or "Intuitions," namely, *time* and *space*. See The Transcendental Aesthetic section of the *Critique of Pure Reason* (1781).

4. *An Interpretation of Christian Ethics* New York: Living Age Books, 1956, p. 61 *passim*. The substance of this volume was presented as the Rauschenbusch Memorial Lectures at the Colgate-Rochester Divinity School in 1934 and published by Harper Brothers in 1935.

5. The context is his play "No Exit" as quoted in *Voix du Siecle* edited by E. Smith and J. Savacoal, New York: Harcourt, Brace and Company, 1960, p. 93. Sartre's discussion of freedom and responsibility is important for understanding "The Life of Love." See further, his famous 1946 lecture published as *Existentialism and Humanism* translation and introduction by Philip Mairet, Brooklyn: Haskell House, 1977.

6. New York: Grove Press, 1954.

7. George F. Macleod, *Only One Way Left—Church Prospect* Glasgow: The Iona Community, nd., p. 38.

CHAPTER X
SPEAKING THE TRUTH IN LOVE

1. *Beyond Tragedy—Essays on the Christian Interpretation of History* New York: Charles Scribner's Sons, 1937, pp. 73-87.
2. I might add that from this idea of a "lying spirit" the idea of Satan later emerged in the biblical record. (See Zechariah 3:1-2 and Job, chapters 1 & 2)

CHAPTER XI
THE GOSPEL IN MINIATURE

1. Material taken from various *Los Angeles Times* articles, 2/14/92 Orange County Edition, Metro; B.4..1; 5/30/91 Orange County Edition, Metro; B.1.2. Since the sermon was delivered, I have no idea of the whereabouts or recent developments in the case of Rollen Stewart.
2. Isaiah 40:7f., cf. I Peter 1:24ff. and John 4:14.
3. See James Pritchard, ed., *Archaeology and the Old Testament* Princeton: Princeton University Press, 1958, p. 183.
4. Genesis 3:22. Moreover, as you'll recall, God put a curse on the snake too.
5. Luke 5:31, Mark 2:17, Matthew 9:12. Consider also his statement, "Physician, heal yourself!"—*iatre therapeuson seauton. Iatros or physician, iatric or pertaining to physicians or medical treatment and iatrikos—healing.* Ignatius to the Ephesians 7:2. See also Eusebius, *Ecclesiastical History* 10.4.11, who describes Jesus like Hippocrates, founder of Greek medicine, "He was like some excellent physician, who, in order to cure the sick, examines what is repulsive, handles sores, and reaps pain himself from the sufferings of others." William Barclay, *New Testament Words* Philadelphia: Westminster Press, 1964, p. 278.

EPILOGUE
THE FINAL FORM OF LOVE...FORGIVENESS

1. *The Irony of American History* New York: Charles Scribner's Sons, 1952, p. 63. Wrote Niebuhr elsewhere in a chapter entitled, "Love as Forgiveness," —"The crown of Christian ethics is the doctrine of forgiveness. In it the whole genius of prophetic religion is expressed. Love as forgiveness is the most difficult and impossible of moral achievements. Yet it is a possibility if the impossibility of love is recognized and the sin in the self is acknowledged. Therefore an ethic culminating in an impossible possibility produces its choicest fruit in terms of the doctrine of forgiveness, the demand that the evil in the other shall be borne without vindictiveness because the evil in the self is known. Forgiveness is a moral achievement which is

possible only when morality is transcended in religion." The chapter and the book concluded, "Nothing short of the knowledge of the true God will save (us) from the impiety of making (ourselves) God and the cruelty of seeing (our) fellow (human beings) as devils, because (we) are involved in the same pretension."

I have personalized this quotation taken from *An Interpretation of Christian Ethics* originally published in 1934, New York: Meridian Books, Living Age Edition, 1960, pp. 201, 213.

In a debate with Paul Ramsey, Prof. Niebuhr said he had "disavowed some of (his) ideas and amended others in later works....I am not therefore able to defend, or interested in defending, any position I took in *An Interpretation of Christian Ethics.*" See Niebuhr's "Reply to Ramsey," *Reinhold Niebuhr: His Religious, Social and Political Thought* edited by Kegley and Bretall, New York: Macmillan, 1956, pp. 434-435. Nevertheless, I find it hard to believe that he would alter or abandon his view that "the final form of love is forgiveness."

2. We would do well to note, for example, Dr. Karl Menninger's abhorrence of violence and vengeance as manifested in corporal and capital punishment, and how revenge can be seen in alcoholism, suicide, sexual crimes as well as child-rearing methods. See in particular "Vengeance is Mine, Saith the Lord," *The Crime of Punishment* New York: Viking, 1966, pp. 190-217. For a brief introduction to Karl Menninger, you might consult my recent article, "The Power of Prevention," *Journal of Emotional and Behavioral Problems* I:4, Winter, 1993, pp. 44-47.

3. I wish I could recall who inferred that if this foundation principle of Western jurisprudence, namely that the punishment must fit the crime, was practiced literally, it would lead inevitably to a blind and toothless world.

4. "You Are Accepted," *The Shaking of the Foundations* New York: Charles Scribner's Sons, 1948, pp. 153-163.

5. Wrote Jan Morris, "For near the heart of the Oxford ethos lies the grand and comforting truth that there is no norm. We are all different; none of us is *entirely* wrong; to understand is to forgive." *Conundrum* New York: Harcourt Brace Jovanovich, Inc., 1974, p. 27.

6. *Black Lamb and Grey Falcon—A Journey Through Yugoslavia*, p. 21.

7. Niebuhr quoted a caveat of G.K. Chesterton (1874-1936) that serves us well, "that tolerance is the virtue of people who do not believe in anything as fairly true." *An Interpretation of Christian Ethics*, p. 204.

8. Louis P. Lochner, *What About Germany?* New York: Dodd, Mead & Co., 1942, p. 2. The reference was suggested by Hagop, a staff member of the National Association for Armenian Studies and Research, Belmont, Massachusetts.

9. As a boy, probably in sixth or seventh grade, I read a book entitled *Armenian Massacres or The Sword of Mohammed containing a complete and*

148

thrilling account of the terrible atrocities and wholesale murders committed in Armenia by Mohammedan Fanatics by Frederick Davis Greene to which is added *The Mohammedan Reign of Terror in Armenia* edited by Henry D. Northrop, Philadelphia: International Publishing Co., 1896.

10. See R.H. Bainton *Hunted Heretic—The Life and Death of Michael Servetus 1511-1533* Boston: Beacon Press, 1953. Calvin himself came to court and called Servetus' ideas "partly impious blasphemies, partly profane and insane errors, and wholly foreign to the Word of God and the orthodox faith." Reginald Manwell and Sophia Taks, *The Church Across the Street* Boston: Beacon, 1963, p. 63.

11. As adapted from Ephraim Emerton, "Calvin and Servetus," *Harvard Theological Review* 11 (2), 1909, pp. 139-160.

12. Romans 12:14, 17-21. I deleted the "heaping of burning coals" only because it described the Vengeance of God which in no way can be compared to anything we could do to avenge ourselves. See Deuteronomy 32:35, Hebrews 10:30 and Proverbs 25:21-22. What is important is seeking to overcome evil with good and leaving vengeance to God. Wrote Chesterton in *What's Wrong with the World*, "The Christian ideal," it is said, "has not been tried and found wanting; it has been found difficult and left untried." Part I, Chapter 5.

ABOUT THE AUTHOR
Robert R. Gillogly

The author is presently Senior Pastor/Head of Staff at First Federated Church (Presbyterian Church U.S.A. and United Church of Christ) in Peoria, Illinois. In addition to earlier pastorates in Massachusetts, Ohio and California, Dr. Gillogly has held positions in the field of education and child care administration. Prior to his present position he was Associate Professor of Philosophy and Religious Studies and Minister to the College at his alma mater, Monmouth College. He is a graduate of Harvard Divinity School and received his Ph.D. from Claremont Graduate School. From 1976-1986 he helped develop and administered a network of children's homes in Kansas and Indiana with The Villages, Inc., an organization founded by the late Dr. Karl Menninger. The author enjoys the romance of ministry and the challenge and repartee involved in preparing and presenting sermons. This volume is his third collection of sermons.